Southern Living
what's for
supper

Six o'Clock
Solutions

30-Minute Meal Plans for
Delicious Weeknight Meals

Oxmoor House®

Spring Greens with Strawberries, page 192

BLT Benedict with Avocado-Tomato Relish, page 185

Pimiento Cheese-Stuffed Burgers, page 84

Mini Berry Cobblers, page 241

contents

welcome

Since the day I began working in the *Southern Living* Test Kitchen nearly 25 years ago, I've always been asked one question: "Do you cook when you get home?" And the answer is YES. My husband and 10-year-old son both love to eat, and cooking has been a passion of mine since I could reach the counter. But, at the end of a long, jam-packed day, sometimes even the thought of preparing a home-cooked dinner for your family can be a challenge. That's why this cookbook is so important to me.

What's for Supper Six o'Clock Solutions is your weekly playbook for creating a successful dinner. Check your pantry list and keep it stocked with convenience items for ready-to-go meals. Keep your thoughts organized with the grocery guide designed to make sure you have everything you need. Plus, my Stretch-Your-Budget tips show you how to use everything in your refrigerator. You'll find some of my favorite *Southern Living* recipes like the Grilled Flank Steak Fajitas (page 18) and my son's pick, Pimiento Cheese-Stuffed Burgers (page 84). And, there's just something luxurious about ending supper during the week with a melt-in-your-mouth dessert—my husband would suggest the Key Lime Pie (page 228).

Sitting down as a family for dinner gets even easier with the *Superfast Suppers,* which are ready in 30 minutes or less. Now that's fast food! Quick entertaining during the week has never been more doable than with the *Company's Coming* chapter. And, for those extra-busy nights when you just have time to pop something in the oven or flip on the slow cooker, there are the *Make-Ahead Magic* recipes.

Like many of you, I'm a working mom who wants to make sure we eat a healthy meal at home, and this book is a great guide. You can make cooking and eating a meal together a welcome event at the end of the long day. In fact, my passion for cooking has been inspired even more by my son who now loves to help me cook in the kitchen.

Vanessa McNeil Rocchio

Vanessa McNeil Rocchio
Southern Living Test Kitchen

weeknight dinner playbook

Every cook needs a well-stocked kitchen.
Shop smart with these checklists for essential
ingredients—and even discover a grocery
guide for five different weeks of meals.

Recipe

TITLE Waffles Benedict

NOTES

PR
TOTAL

INGREDIENTS
2 cups baking mix
1⅓ cups buttermilk
½ cup parmesan
2 Tbsp. vegetable oil
5 eggs
½ tsp. white vinegar

1 pkg. hollandaise sa.
1 Tbsp. lemon juice
¼ tsp. dried tarragon
8 prosciutto slices
fresh chives for garnish

GROCERY LIST
- BUTTERMILK
- PARMESAN
- EGGS
- TARRAGON
- PROSCIUT...

pantry planner

Use this list to stock up on the basics for quick and easy cooking. If you keep these items on hand, you'll be able to make most of the recipes in this book. Plus, you won't have to stop at the grocery store each night wondering what you can cook for dinner.

Oils, Vinegars, and Condiments

Alfredo sauce
Barbecue sauce
Canola or vegetable oil
Capers
Cooking spray
Dressings: blue cheese, honey-mustard, Ranch, Thousand Island
Dry wine: red, white
Honey
Hot sauce
Ketchup
Mayonnaise
Mustards: Dijon, spicy brown, whole grain, yellow
Olive oil
Pasta sauce
Peanut butter
Peanut oil
Pizza sauce
Salsa
Sesame oil
Soy sauce: lite and regular
Vinegars: apple cider, balsamic, red wine, sherry, white wine
Worcestershire sauce

Grains, Pastas, and More

Couscous
Dried breadcrumbs: plain and Italian-seasoned
Egg noodles
Fettuccine, rotini, and spaghetti
Flour tortillas
Panko breadcrumbs
Quick-cooking grits
Quick-cooking barley
Quick-cooking oats
Rice
Rice noodles
Self-rising cornmeal mixes

Baking Essentials

All-purpose flour
All-purpose baking mix
Baking powder
Baking soda
Brown sugar: light and dark
Brownie mix
Cornstarch
Pecans
Powdered sugar
Self-rising flour
Semisweet chocolate morsels
Granulated sugar
Vanilla extract

Canned Goods

Artichoke hearts
Beans: white, black, pinto
Black-eyed peas
Broth: beef, chicken, vegetable
Chipotle peppers in adobo sauce
Chopped green chiles
Corn: cream-style and whole kernel
Diced tomatoes and green chiles
Diced pimiento
Enchilada sauce
Roasted red peppers
Sliced mushrooms
Soups: cream of celery, cream of chicken, cream of mushroom
Tomatoes: diced, plain, seasoned

Spice Rack

Bay leaves
Black peppercorns (grind fresh)
Bouillon granules
Chili powder
Curry powder
Dried basil
Dried dill weed
Dried oregano
Dried rosemary
Dried thyme
Dry mustard
Garlic powder
Garlic salt
Ground cinnamon
Ground cumin
Ground ginger
Ground nutmeg
Kosher salt
Onion powder
Paprika
Ranch dressing mix
Red pepper: crushed and ground
Salt
Seasoned pepper
Seasoning blends: Asian, Cajun, Italian, Mediterranean, Mexican, Sesame seeds
Taco seasoning mix
White pepper

fridge & freezer mainstays

Set aside a convenient time each week to plan your meals and make your grocery list. Our Weekly Meal Planner on page 12 makes it easy with five weeks worth of meal plans. Or, if it's easier to shop for one night at a time, each recipe contains its own grocery list of non-staple items.

Refrigerator

Bacon
Bagged carrots
Bagged lettuce
Broccoli florets
Butter
Diced tomatoes
Eggs
Grated Parmesan cheese
Jarred minced garlic
Mashed potatoes
Milk
Pizza dough
Prechopped onion
Prechopped veggies
Precooked chicken:
  chopped, shredded,
  sliced
Preshredded cheese
Refrigerated pesto
Refrigerated piecrusts
Sour cream
Yogurt

Freezer

Frozen corn
Frozen fish
Frozen fruit
Frozen hash browns
Frozen mixed vegetables
Frozen peas
Frozen spinach
Ice cream, sherbet

weekly meal planner

Planning nutritious, hearty meals takes time, so we've made it easy for you by putting together five weeks of menus, complete with grocery-shopping lists! Simply take the list with you to the grocery store, and you'll have everything you need for a week of delicious eating.

Weeknight Winners

Monday: King Ranch Chicken Mac and Cheese (page 108)

Tuesday: Roast Chicken (page 98)

Wednesday: Spicy Ham-and-Greens Quiche (page 180)

Thursday: Shrimp Destin Linguine (page 40)

Friday: Simple Meatloaf (page 127)

check staples

- ❏ 1 (10 ¾-oz.) can cream of chicken soup
- ❏ 1 (10-oz.) can diced tomatoes and green chiles
- ❏ All-purpose baking mix
- ❏ Black pepper
- ❏ Brown sugar
- ❏ Butter
- ❏ Chili powder
- ❏ Dried rosemary
- ❏ Dry white wine
- ❏ Eggs
- ❏ Ground cumin
- ❏ Ketchup
- ❏ Milk
- ❏ Olive oil
- ❏ Quick-cooking oats
- ❏ Seasoned pepper
- ❏ Yellow mustard

produce

- ❏ Green onions
- ❏ 1 small garlic bulb
- ❏ 2 lemons
- ❏ 1 bunch fresh parsley
- ❏ 1 bunch fresh dill weed
- ❏ 2 medium onions
- ❏ 1 green bell pepper

refrigerated

- ❏ 1 (9-oz.) package refrigerated linguine
- ❏ Sour cream
- ❏ 6 oz. shredded Cheddar cheese
- ❏ 6 oz. shredded pepper Jack cheese

shellfish, meat & poultry

- ❏ 1 ½ lb. unpeeled, large raw shrimp
- ❏ 1 (4- to 5-lb.) whole chicken
- ❏ 2 lb. chicken breasts
- ❏ 1 ½ lb. lean ground beef

deli

- ❏ Baked ham

pantry items

- ❏ 1 (16-oz.) package cellentani pasta
- ❏ 1 (6-oz.) tube pasteurized processed cheese food

frozen

- ❏ 1 (16-oz.) package frozen chopped collard greens

Superfast Suppers

Monday: Chicken with Ratatouille (page 32)

Tuesday: Roasted Vegetable Sandwiches (page 66)

Wednesday: Easy Lasagna (page 90)

Thursday: BLT Salad (page 56)

Friday: Pimiento Cheese-Stuffed Burgers (page 84)

check staples

- ❏ Butter
- ❏ Canola oil
- ❏ Eggs
- ❏ Flour
- ❏ Ketchup
- ❏ Mayonnaise
- ❏ Mustard
- ❏ Olive oil
- ❏ 2 (26-oz.) jars pasta sauce
- ❏ Black pepper
- ❏ Refrigerated ready-made pesto
- ❏ Table salt

produce

- ❏ 2 small red onions
- ❏ 2 medium-size sweet onions
- ❏ 2 eggplants
- ❏ 2 medium zucchini (about 1 lb.)
- ❏ 5 small yellow summer squash
- ❏ 1 small garlic bulb
- ❏ 2 medium-size red bell peppers
- ❏ 1 medium tomato
- ❏ 2 bunches fresh basil
- ❏ 1 bunch fresh parsley
- ❏ 1 lemon
- ❏ 1 lb. assorted heirloom tomatoes
- ❏ 1 (5-oz.) package arugula
- ❏ Lettuce leaves

refrigerated

- ❏ 4 provolone cheese slices
- ❏ 1 (15-oz.) container part-skim ricotta cheese
- ❏ 1 (16-oz.) package shredded Italian three-cheese blend or mozzarella cheese

meat & poultry

- ❏ 6 (4-oz.) chicken breast cutlets
- ❏ 1 lb. mild Italian sausage
- ❏ Thick applewood-smoked bacon
- ❏ 2 lb. ground chuck

deli

- ❏ Pimiento cheese

pantry items

- ❏ Dried Italian seasoning
- ❏ No-boil lasagna noodles

bakery

- ❏ 4 French hamburger buns
- ❏ Hamburger buns
- ❏ 1 artisan bread loaf

Classic Comforts

Monday: **Pancakes with Buttered Honey Syrup (page 186)**

Tuesday: **Italian Meatballs (page 86)**

Wednesday: **Slaw Reubens (page 65)**

Thursday: **Noodle-and-Spinach Casserole (page 131)**

Friday: **Shrimp and Grits (page 41)**

check staples

- ❏ Baking powder
- ❏ Baking soda
- ❏ Barbecue sauce
- ❏ Black pepper
- ❏ Butter
- ❏ Chicken broth
- ❏ Egg noodles
- ❏ Eggs
- ❏ Flour
- ❏ Garlic salt
- ❏ Hot sauce
- ❏ Italian-seasoned breadcrumbs
- ❏ Olive oil
- ❏ I (26-oz.) jar spaghetti sauce
- ❏ Quick-cooking grits
- ❏ Rice
- ❏ Soy sauce
- ❏ Spicy brown mustard
- ❏ Sugar
- ❏ Table salt
- ❏ Thousand Island dressing
- ❏ Vegetable cooking spray
- ❏ White wine vinegar

produce

- ❏ I lemon
- ❏ I Granny Smith apple
- ❏ I bunch fresh flat-leaf parsley
- ❏ shredded coleslaw mix
- ❏ I small garlic bulb
- ❏ I package fresh baby spinach

refrigerated

- ❏ I pt. buttermilk
- ❏ Freshly grated Parmesan cheese
- ❏ Swiss cheese slices
- ❏ 8 oz. shredded Monterey Jack cheese
- ❏ Sour cream

shellfish, meat & poultry

- ❏ I lb. unpeeled, medium-size raw shrimp
- ❏ 3 ½ lb. ground beef

pantry items

- ❏ Fennel seeds
- ❏ Italian seasoning

bakery

- ❏ Sandwich buns (optional)
- ❏ I rye or pumpernickel bread loaf

deli

- ❏ I (7-oz.) package roast beef

frozen

- ❏ I (10-oz.) package frozen chopped spinach

Farmer's Market Favorites

Monday: **Asian Beef Salad (page 58)**

Tuesday: **Poblano Chicken Tacos (page 102)**

Wednesday: **Greek Salsa Salad with Grouper (page 38)**

Thursday: **Peach-and-Tomato Gazpacho with Cucumber Yogurt (page 53)**

Friday: **Peach and Pork Kabobs (page 89)**

check staples

- ❏ Apple cider vinegar
- ❏ Asian garlic-chile sauce
- ❏ Barbecue sauce
- ❏ Black pepper
- ❏ Butter
- ❏ Light brown sugar
- ❏ Lite soy sauce
- ❏ Minced garlic
- ❏ Olive oil
- ❏ Sesame oil
- ❏ Table salt
- ❏ Teriyaki sauce
- ❏ White pepper

produce

- ❏ 1 head napa cabbage
- ❏ 1 large head romaine lettuce
- ❏ 1 medium-size sweet onion
- ❏ 7 large tomatoes
- ❏ 5 cucumbers
- ❏ 1 cup grape tomatoes
- ❏ 7 large peaches
- ❏ 1 large green bell pepper
- ❏ 1 (8-oz.) container refrigerated chopped assorted bell peppers
- ❏ 2 small red onions
- ❏ 1 small garlic bulb
- ❏ 1 (3-oz.) container refrigerated sliced green onions
- ❏ 1 bunch fresh cilantro
- ❏ 5 limes
- ❏ 2 lemons
- ❏ 1 bunch fresh rosemary
- ❏ 1 large poblano pepper
- ❏ 1 (5-oz.) container mixed salad greens with herbs
- ❏ Fresh chives

refrigerated

- ❏ Greek vinaigrette with feta cheese and garlic
- ❏ Plain Greek yogurt

shellfish, meat & poultry

- ❏ 1 ½ lb. steamed grouper fillets
- ❏ 2 (1-lb.) flank steaks
- ❏ 1 ½ lb. chicken
- ❏ 1 lb. boneless pork loin

pantry items

- ❏ Metal skewers
- ❏ Mango-lime seafood seasoning
- ❏ 12 (6-inch) fajita-size corn tortillas
- ❏ Bourbon

bakery

- ❏ 1 round artisan bread loaf

Everyday Easy

Monday: White Lightning Chicken Chili (page 106)

Tuesday: Taco Salad (page 87)

Wednesday: Garden Tomato Sauce over Pasta (page 121)

Thursday: Grilled Scallop Kabobs (page 42)

Friday: Chicken Tetrazzini (page 140)

check staples

- ❑ 1 (10 ¾-oz.) can cream of mushroom soup
- ❑ 1 (10 ¾-oz.) can cream of chicken soup
- ❑ 1 (10 ¾-oz.) can cream of celery soup
- ❑ 1 (6-oz.) jar sliced mushrooms
- ❑ 2 (4.5-oz.) cans chopped green chiles

- ❑ Black pepper
- ❑ Chicken broth
- ❑ Dry red wine
- ❑ Kosher salt
- ❑ Olive oil
- ❑ Pasta
- ❑ Table salt
- ❑ Taco seasoning mix

produce

- ❑ 2 large sweet onions
- ❑ 1 small garlic bulb
- ❑ 3 large avocados
- ❑ 1 mango
- ❑ 2 small red onions
- ❑ 1 bunch fresh cilantro
- ❑ 3 limes
- ❑ 2 lemons
- ❑ 1 head iceberg lettuce
- ❑ 1 tomato

- ❑ 4 medium-size heirloom tomatoes
- ❑ 1 package fresh oregano or marjoram
- ❑ 20 thick asparagus spears

refrigerated

- ❑ Sour cream
- ❑ Shredded Monterey Jack cheese
- ❑ Shredded Parmesan cheese
- ❑ Shredded Cheddar cheese

shellfish, meat & poultry

- ❑ 40 sea scallops
- ❑ Chicken
- ❑ 1 lb. lean ground beef
- ❑ Bacon

pantry items

- ❑ 1 (1.25-oz.) envelope white chicken chili seasoning mix
- ❑ 1 (16-oz.) jar medium salsa
- ❑ Bite-size tortilla chips
- ❑ 1 (16-oz.) package vermicelli
- ❑ 3 (15-oz.) cans navy beans
- ❑ 1 (16-oz.) can kidney beans
- ❑ Herb-flavored olive oil

superfast
suppers

Go from grocery bag to dinner
table in just a half an hour
with these tasty recipes.

Grilled Flank Steak Fajitas

MAKES: 4 SERVINGS   **HANDS-ON TIME: 30 MIN.**
TOTAL TIME: 30 MIN.

1½ Tbsp. canola oil, divided	¼ cup chopped fresh cilantro
1 tsp. chili powder	8 (6-inch) fajita-size flour
1 tsp. ground cumin	tortillas, warmed
1 tsp. table salt, divided	1 (7-oz.) package refrigerated
¾ tsp. freshly ground black	guacamole
pepper, divided	½ cup (2 oz.) crumbled queso
1 (1½-lb.) flank steak	fresco (fresh Mexican
1 (14.4-oz.) package frozen	cheese)
pepper stir-fry with onion	

1. Preheat grill to 350° to 400° (medium-high) heat. Stir together 1 Tbsp. oil, chili powder, cumin, ½ tsp. salt, and ½ tsp. black pepper; rub over steak.

2. Grill steak, covered with grill lid, 8 minutes on each side or to desired degree of doneness. Let stand 10 minutes.

3. Meanwhile, heat remaining ½ Tbsp. oil in a large skillet over medium-high heat. Add frozen vegetables, remaining ½ tsp. salt, and ¼ tsp. black pepper; sauté 6 minutes. Stir in cilantro; sauté 2 minutes.

4. Cut steak diagonally across the grain into thin strips. Serve steak and vegetables with warm tortillas, guacamole, and cheese.

Vanessa's Savvy Secret: Use frozen bell pepper mix to make a quick and easy topping for these fajitas. No cutting or thawing required. Just toss the peppers in the skillet and sauté!

grocery guide:

- ❏ 1 (1½-lb.) flank steak
- ❏ 1 (14.4-oz.) package frozen pepper stir-fry with onion
- ❏ 1 bunch fresh cilantro
- ❏ 1 (7-oz.) package refrigerated guacamole
- ❏ 1 package crumbled queso fresco (fresh Mexican cheese)

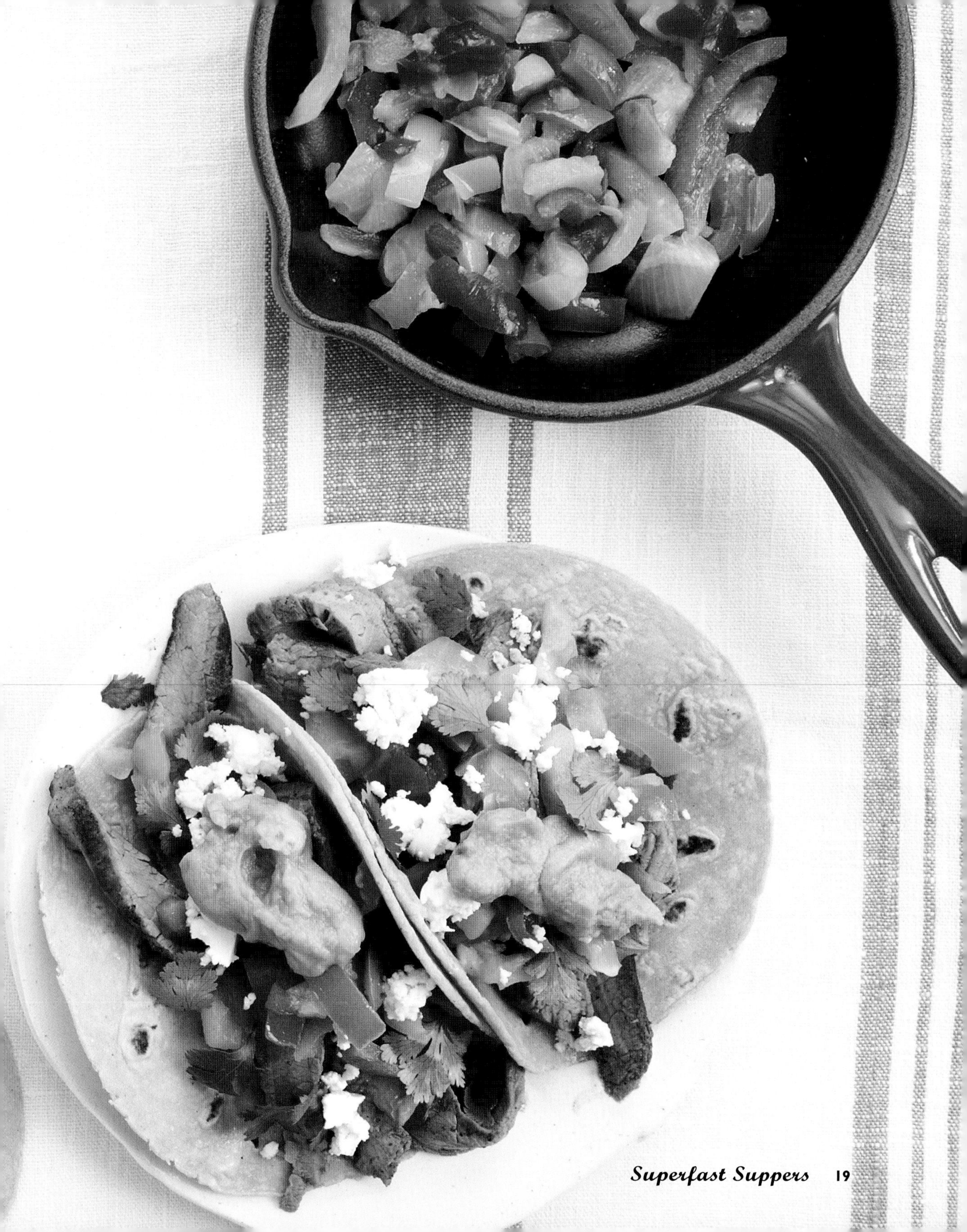

Skillet Shepherd's Pie

MAKES: 4 SERVINGS **HANDS-ON TIME: 21 MIN.**
TOTAL TIME: 21 MIN.

Packaged products and a one-pot method make this hearty meal a weeknight staple.

1	lb. ground round
¾	cup chopped onion
2	garlic cloves, minced
2	Tbsp. all-purpose flour
¾	cup beef broth
1	Tbsp. tomato paste
½	tsp. table salt
½	tsp. freshly ground black pepper
2	tsp. chopped fresh thyme
1	cup frozen peas and carrots
1	(24-oz.) package refrigerated mashed potatoes
¾	cup (3 oz.) shredded sharp Cheddar cheese

1. Cook ground beef, onion, and garlic in a medium-size nonstick skillet over medium-high heat, stirring often, 5 minutes until meat crumbles and is no longer pink; drain and return to skillet.

2. Sprinkle beef mixture with flour; cook, stirring constantly, 1 minute. Add broth and next 4 ingredients, stirring until blended. Stir in peas and carrots; bring to a boil. Cover, reduce heat to low, and simmer, stirring occasionally, 10 minutes or until slightly thickened.

3. Meanwhile, heat mashed potatoes according to package directions.

4. Spoon mashed potatoes over beef mixture, spreading almost to edge of skillet; sprinkle with cheese. Cover and simmer 2 minutes or until cheese melts.

grocery guide:

❑ 1 lb. ground round
❑ 1 medium onion
❑ 1 small garlic bulb
❑ 1 (6-oz.) can tomato paste
❑ 1 bunch fresh thyme
❑ 1 (16-oz.) package frozen peas and carrots

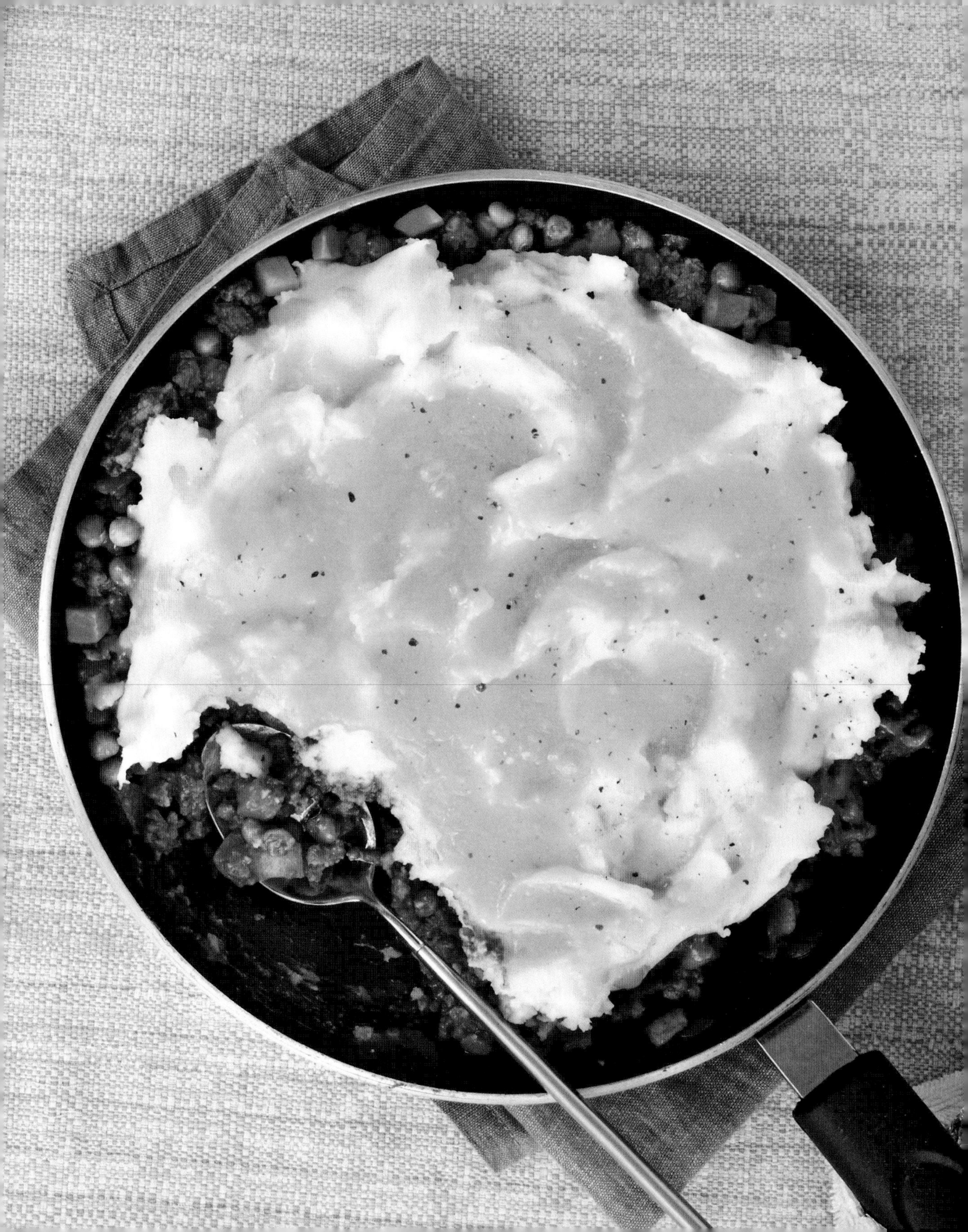

Bacon Cheeseburger Pizza

MAKES: 4 SERVINGS   **HANDS-ON TIME: 10 MIN.**
TOTAL TIME: 30 MIN.

Perfect for busy weeknights, this quick meal combines two family favorites—burgers and pizza. Be sure to take advantage of time-savers like shredded cheese and cooked bacon to get dinner on the table in 30 minutes.

¼ cup mayonnaise	1 lb. fresh bakery pizza dough
¼ cup dill pickle relish	1 ½ cups (6 oz.) shredded
1 Tbsp. French dressing	Cheddar cheese
1 ½ tsp. dried minced onion	6 fully-cooked bacon slices,
1 lb. ground round	crumbled
½ cup thinly sliced onion	1 cup shredded iceberg lettuce
½ cup ketchup	½ cup chopped tomato
1 Tbsp. yellow mustard	

1. Preheat oven to 450°. Stir together first 4 ingredients in a small bowl.

2. Cook ground beef and sliced onion in a medium-size nonstick skillet over medium-high heat, stirring often, 5 minutes or until meat crumbles and is no longer pink; drain and return to skillet. Stir in ketchup and mustard.

3. Roll dough into a 12-inch circle on a lightly floured surface; place on a lightly greased baking sheet. Spread mayonnaise mixture over dough, leaving a 1-inch border. Top with beef mixture, cheese, and bacon. Bake at 450° for 19 to 20 minutes or until crust is golden and cheese is bubbly. Remove from oven; let stand 5 minutes. Top with lettuce and tomato.

Vanessa's Savvy Secret: Taking the pizza dough out of the fridge 30 minutes before you plan to use it makes it easier to knead.

grocery guide:

- ❏ 1 (9-oz.) jar dill pickle relish
- ❏ 1 (8-oz.) jar French dressing
- ❏ 1 (1.88-oz.) jar dried minced onion
- ❏ 1 lb. ground round
- ❏ 1 medium onion
- ❏ 1 (2.52-oz.) package fully-cooked bacon
- ❏ 1 head iceberg lettuce
- ❏ 1 tomato

Lemon Pork Chops with Quinoa Salad

MAKES: 6 SERVINGS
TOTAL TIME: 35 MIN.
HANDS-ON TIME: 25 MIN.

6   (½-inch-thick) bone-in center-cut pork rib chops (about 4 lb.)
2   Tbsp. lemon-herb seasoning
1 ¾ tsp. kosher salt, divided
6   Tbsp. olive oil, divided
1 ½ cups uncooked quinoa
1   (8-oz.) package fresh sugar snap peas
1   garlic clove, sliced
     Lemon-Garlic Vinaigrette
⅓   cup loosely packed fresh flat-leaf parsley leaves
¼   cup chopped dry-roasted almonds

1. Rub pork chops with herb seasoning and 1 tsp. kosher salt. Sear half of pork in 2 ½ Tbsp. hot olive oil in a large skillet over medium-high heat 4 to 5 minutes on each side or until browned and cooked through. Keep pork warm on a wire rack in a 200° oven. Repeat procedure with 2 ½ Tbsp. olive oil and remaining pork. Wipe skillet clean.

2. Bring quinoa, ½ tsp. kosher salt, and 4 cups water to a boil in large saucepan over high heat. Cover, reduce heat to medium-low, and simmer 8 to 10 minutes or until tender; drain. Return to saucepan; cover. Let stand 10 minutes.

3. Cut sugar snap peas in half crosswise. Heat remaining 1 Tbsp. olive oil in skillet over medium-high heat; cook peas in hot oil 1 minute or until bright green and tender. Sprinkle with remaining ¼ tsp. salt. Add garlic; sauté 1 minute. Remove from heat.

4. Fluff quinoa with a fork. Add quinoa and Lemon-Garlic Vinaigrette to sugar snap pea mixture, and toss to coat. Stir in parsley and almonds. Serve with pork.

Lemon-Garlic Vinaigrette

Whisk together 2 Tbsp. lemon juice; 1 Tbsp. olive oil; 2 garlic cloves, minced; ¼ tsp. kosher salt; and ¼ tsp. black pepper.

grocery guide:

- ❑ 6 (½-inch-thick) bone-in center-cut pork rib chops (about 4 lb.)
- ❑ 1 (3-oz.) jar lemon-herb seasoning
- ❑ 1 ½ cups quinoa
- ❑ 1 (8-oz.) package fresh sugar snap peas
- ❑ 1 lemon
- ❑ 1 small garlic bulb
- ❑ 1 bunch fresh flat-leaf parsley leaves
- ❑ 1 (11-oz.) can dry-roasted almonds

Dirty Rice

MAKES: 4 SERVINGS **HANDS-ON TIME: 28 MIN.**
TOTAL TIME: 28 MIN.

2	(3.5-oz.) bags boil-in-bag white rice	½	cup chopped red bell pepper
2	(I-lb.) packages hot ground pork sausage	½	cup chopped celery
I	cup chopped onion	2	garlic cloves, minced
½	cup chopped green bell pepper	¼	cup chopped fresh parsley
		½	tsp. table salt
		¼	tsp. ground red pepper

1. Prepare rice according to package directions; drain.

2. Meanwhile, brown sausage in a large nonstick skillet over medium-high heat, stirring often, 8 minutes or until sausage crumbles and is no longer pink. Add onion and next 4 ingredients; cook, stirring often, 12 minutes or until vegetables are tender. Remove from heat; stir in rice, parsley, salt, and ground red pepper.

Kid Flip: Use mild sausage and cut back on the ground red pepper for family members who are sensitive to spicy foods.

grocery guide:

- ❏ 2 (I-lb.) packages hot ground pork sausage
- ❏ I medium onion
- ❏ I green bell pepper
- ❏ I red bell pepper
- ❏ I bunch celery
- ❏ I small garlic bulb
- ❏ I bunch fresh flat-leaf parsley

Chicken Marsala

MAKES: 4 TO 6 SERVINGS　　**HANDS-ON TIME: 26 MIN.**
TOTAL TIME: 26 MIN.

Serve this classic chicken dish over mashed potatoes
or with pasta.

1½ lb. chicken breast cutlets	⅔ cup Marsala
6 Tbsp. all-purpose flour	½ cup heavy cream
1 (10 ½-oz.) can condensed beef broth, undiluted	½ tsp. table salt
5 Tbsp. butter, divided	½ tsp. freshly ground black pepper
1½ cups sliced fresh mushrooms	¼ cup coarsely chopped fresh flat-leaf parsley

1. Dredge chicken in 5 Tbsp. flour. Whisk together remaining 1 Tbsp.
flour and beef broth in a small bowl.

2. Melt 1 Tbsp. butter in a large nonstick skillet over medium heat.
Add mushrooms; sauté 6 minutes, stirring once, until browned.
Transfer mushrooms to a bowl.

3. Add 2 Tbsp. butter to skillet over medium-high heat. Add half of
chicken; cook 2 to 3 minutes on each side or until done. Remove from
skillet; keep warm. Repeat procedure with remaining butter and
chicken cutlets.

4. Add Marsala to skillet, stirring to loosen browned bits from bottom
of skillet. Add broth mixture, cream, salt, and black pepper; bring to a
boil, stirring constantly. Return mushrooms to skillet. Reduce heat,
and simmer, stirring often, 3 minutes or until thickened. Return chicken
to skillet, turning to coat; cook 1 minute. Remove from heat; sprinkle
with parsley.

grocery guide:

- ❏ 1 ½ lb. chicken breast cutlets
- ❏ 1 (10 ½-oz.) can condensed beef broth
- ❏ 1 (8-oz.) package sliced fresh mushrooms
- ❏ 1 (750-milliliter) bottle Marsala
- ❏ 1 (8-oz.) container heavy cream
- ❏ 1 bunch fresh flat-leaf parsley

Pan-Grilled Chicken with Fresh Plum Salsa

MAKES: 4 SERVINGS   **HANDS-ON TIME: 26 MIN.**
TOTAL TIME: 26 MIN.

1 cup chopped ripe plums (about 2 plums)	2 tsp. fresh lime juice
1 small jalapeño pepper, seeded and diced	¾ tsp. table salt, divided
2 Tbsp. chopped fresh basil	2 Tbsp. brown sugar
2 Tbsp. chopped red onion	½ tsp. ground cumin
	4 (4-oz.) chicken breast cutlets
	2 tsp. olive oil

1. Stir together plums, next 4 ingredients, and ¼ tsp. table salt in a medium bowl.

2. Stir together brown sugar, cumin, and remaining ½ tsp. salt in a small bowl. Rub chicken with brown sugar mixture.

3. Cook chicken in hot oil in a grill pan or nonstick skillet over medium heat 3 minutes on each side or until done. Serve with plum mixture.

Vanessa's Savvy Secret:
If you have chicken breasts on hand, pound them very thin to use in this recipe.

grocery guide:
- ❏ 2 ripe plums
- ❏ 1 small jalapeño pepper
- ❏ 1 bunch fresh basil
- ❏ 1 small red onion
- ❏ 1 lime
- ❏ 1 lb. chicken breast cutlets

Chicken with Ratatouille

grocery guide:
- ❏ I small red onion
- ❏ I (I-lb.) eggplant
- ❏ 2 small yellow squash
- ❏ I small garlic bulb
- ❏ I medium-size red bell pepper
- ❏ I medium tomato
- ❏ I bunch fresh basil
- ❏ I ½ lb. chicken breast cutlets

MAKES: 6 SERVINGS   **HANDS-ON TIME: 30 MIN.**
TOTAL TIME: 30 MIN.

I small red onion, chopped	¼ cup chopped fresh basil
½ (I-lb.) eggplant, peeled and chopped	I ¼ tsp. kosher salt, divided
2 Tbsp. olive oil	¾ tsp. freshly ground black pepper, divided
2 small yellow squash, chopped	6 (4-oz.) chicken breast cutlets
2 garlic cloves, minced	⅓ cup all-purpose flour
I medium-size red bell pepper, chopped	I cup canola oil
I medium tomato, diced	Garnish: fresh basil leaves

1. Sauté onion and eggplant in hot olive oil in a large nonstick skillet over medium-high heat 5 minutes or until tender and light brown around edges. Add squash, garlic, and bell pepper; sauté 5 minutes or until tender. Add tomato, basil, and ¼ tsp. each kosher salt and freshly ground black pepper. Cook, stirring constantly, 2 to 3 minutes or until mixture is thoroughly heated.

2. Remove vegetable mixture from skillet. Cover loosely with aluminum foil to keep warm. Wipe skillet clean.

3. Rinse chicken, and pat dry. Sprinkle with remaining I tsp. salt and remaining ½ tsp. pepper. Dredge chicken in flour, shaking off excess.

4. Fry chicken, in 2 batches, in hot canola oil in skillet over medium-high heat 2 to 3 minutes on each side or until golden brown and done. Drain on a wire rack over paper towels; cover and keep warm. Transfer to a serving dish, and top with vegetable mixture.

Stretch Your Budget: This is the perfect one-dish dinner when the garden is in full swing. Feel free to substitute whatever is overflowing in your garden or at the market for the vegetables in the ratatouille.

Pecan-Crusted Chicken and Tortellini with Herbed Butter Sauce

MAKES: 4 SERVINGS **HANDS-ON TIME: 30 MIN.**
TOTAL TIME: 30 MIN.

2 (9-oz.) packages refrigerated cheese-filled tortellini	3 Tbsp. olive oil
4 (4-oz.) chicken breast cutlets	½ cup butter
½ tsp. table salt	3 garlic cloves, thinly sliced
¼ tsp. freshly ground black pepper	3 Tbsp. chopped fresh basil
¾ cup finely chopped pecans	3 Tbsp. chopped fresh flat-leaf parsley
1 large egg, lightly beaten	¼ cup (1 oz.) freshly shredded Parmesan cheese

1. Prepare tortellini according to package directions; keep warm.

2. Meanwhile, sprinkle chicken with salt and pepper. Place pecans in a shallow bowl. Place egg in a second bowl. Dip chicken in egg, allowing excess to drip off. Dredge chicken in pecans, pressing firmly to adhere.

3. Cook chicken in hot oil in a large nonstick skillet over medium-high heat 2 minutes on each side or until done. Remove from skillet; keep warm. Wipe skillet clean.

4. Melt butter in skillet over medium heat. Add garlic, and sauté 5 to 7 minutes or until garlic is caramel-colored and butter begins to turn golden brown. Immediately remove from heat, and stir in basil, parsley, and hot cooked tortellini. Sprinkle with cheese. Serve immediately with chicken.

Stretch Your Budget: Buy a large block of Parmesan cheese and shred your own. Freeze what you don't need for this recipe to use another time.

grocery guide:
- ❏ 2 (9-oz.) packages refrigerated cheese-filled tortellini
- ❏ 1 lb. chicken breast cutlets
- ❏ 1 small garlic bulb
- ❏ 1 bunch fresh basil
- ❏ 1 bunch fresh flat-leaf parsley

Chicken-and-Veggie Stir-fry

MAKES: 4 SERVINGS   **HANDS-ON TIME: 30 MIN.**
TOTAL TIME: 30 MIN.

This colorful chicken and vegetable stir-fry is a delight for the eyes as well as the taste buds with its colorful array of Broccolini, red bell pepper, yellow squash, and green onions.

1 lb. skinned and boned chicken breasts, cut into thin strips	1 small yellow squash, thinly sliced into half moons
½ tsp. table salt	¼ cup sliced green onions
¼ cup cornstarch	2 tsp. cornstarch
4 Tbsp. vegetable oil, divided	1 Tbsp. fresh lime juice
½ lb. Broccolini, cut into 1-inch pieces	1½ tsp. soy sauce
1 cup chicken broth, divided	1 tsp. Asian chili-garlic sauce
1 red bell pepper, cut into thin strips	Hot cooked rice

1. Sprinkle chicken with salt; toss with ¼ cup cornstarch.

2. Stir-fry chicken in 3 Tbsp. hot oil in a large skillet or wok over medium-high heat 5 to 6 minutes or until golden brown and done. Transfer to a plate, using a slotted spoon; keep warm. Add Broccolini and ¼ cup broth to skillet; cook, covered, 1 to 2 minutes or until crisp-tender. Transfer to plate with chicken, using slotted spoon.

3. Add remaining 1 Tbsp. oil to skillet. Sauté bell pepper and next 2 ingredients in hot oil 2 minutes or until crisp-tender.

4. Whisk together 2 tsp. cornstarch and remaining ¾ cup broth until cornstarch dissolves. Add broth mixture, chicken, and Broccolini (with any accumulated juices) to bell pepper mixture in skillet. Cook, stirring often, 1 minute or until liquid thickens. Stir in lime juice and next 2 ingredients. Serve over hot cooked rice.

grocery guide:

- ❏ 1 lb. skinned and boned chicken breasts
- ❏ 1 bunch Broccolini
- ❏ 1 red bell pepper
- ❏ 1 small yellow squash
- ❏ 1 bunch green onions
- ❏ 1 lime
- ❏ 1 (8-oz.) jar Asian chili-garlic sauce

Greek Salsa Salad with Grouper

MAKES: 4 SERVINGS **HANDS-ON TIME: 15 MIN.**
TOTAL TIME: 15 MIN.

1   (8-oz.) round artisan bread loaf
2   Tbsp. butter, melted
1   tsp. minced garlic
1   (5-oz.) container mixed salad greens with herbs
1 ½ lb. steamed grouper fillets, broken into bite-size pieces
2   large tomatoes, quartered
1   cucumber, seeded and thinly sliced into half moons
1   (8-oz.) container refrigerated chopped tri-colored bell peppers
1   (3-oz.) container refrigerated sliced green onions
1   cup refrigerated Greek vinaigrette with feta cheese and garlic*

1. Preheat oven to 425°. Cut bread into 1-inch cubes (about 2 cups), and place in a single layer on a jelly-roll pan. Combine butter and garlic; drizzle over bread cubes, and toss to coat. Bake 5 to 7 minutes or until lightly toasted, stirring twice. Transfer bread to a wire rack, and cool completely (about 5 minutes).

2. Arrange salad greens and next 5 ingredients on individual serving plates. Top with bread cubes, and serve with vinaigrette.

   * We tested with Marie's Greek Vinaigrette with Feta Cheese & Garlic.

Make It Snappy:
If you have 15 minutes, then you have time to make Greek Salsa Salad with Grouper. Pick up steamed fish from your grocery seafood counter, and create this easy recipe.

grocery guide:

- ❏ 1 (8-oz.) round artisan bread loaf
- ❏ 1 (5-oz.) container mixed salad greens with herbs
- ❏ 1 ½ lb. steamed grouper fillets
- ❏ 2 large tomatoes
- ❏ 1 cucumber
- ❏ 1 (8-oz.) container refrigerated chopped tri-colored bell peppers
- ❏ 1 (3-oz.) container refrigerated sliced green onions
- ❏ 1 (11.5-oz.) bottle refrigerated Greek vinaigrette with feta cheese and garlic

Shrimp Destin Linguine

MAKES: 2 TO 3 SERVINGS   **HANDS-ON TIME: 30 MIN.**
TOTAL TIME: 30 MIN.

1½	lb. unpeeled, large raw shrimp	1	Tbsp. dry white wine
1	(9-oz.) package refrigerated linguine	2	tsp. fresh lemon juice
¼	cup butter	½	tsp. table salt
¼	cup olive oil	¼	tsp. coarsely ground black pepper
¼	cup chopped green onions	1	Tbsp. chopped fresh dill
2	garlic cloves, minced	1	Tbsp. chopped fresh flat-leaf parsley

1. Peel shrimp, leaving tails on, if desired. Devein, if desired.

2. Prepare pasta according to package directions; keep warm.

3. Meanwhile, melt butter with oil in a large skillet over medium-high heat; add green onions and garlic, and sauté 4 to 5 minutes or until onions are tender. Add shrimp, wine, and next 3 ingredients. Cook over medium heat, stirring occasionally, 3 to 5 minutes or just until shrimp turn pink. Stir in dill and parsley. Remove shrimp with a slotted spoon, reserving sauce in skillet.

4. Add hot cooked pasta to sauce in skillet, tossing to coat. Transfer pasta to a serving bowl, and top with shrimp.

Make It Gourmet: For a little kick, add a pinch of dried crushed red pepper just before serving.

grocery guide:

- ❏ 1½ lb. unpeeled, large raw shrimp
- ❏ 1 (9-oz.) package refrigerated linguine
- ❏ 1 bunch green onions
- ❏ 1 small garlic bulb
- ❏ 1 lemon
- ❏ 1 bunch fresh dill
- ❏ 1 bunch fresh flat-leaf parsley

Shrimp and Grits

MAKES: 6 SERVINGS   **HANDS-ON TIME: 25 MIN.**
TOTAL TIME: 30 MIN.

Parmesan Grits:
- ½ tsp. table salt
- 1 cup uncooked quick-cooking grits
- ½ cup freshly grated Parmesan cheese
- ½ tsp. freshly ground black pepper

Creamy Shrimp Sauce:
- 1 lb. unpeeled, medium-size raw shrimp
- ¼ tsp. freshly ground black pepper

- ⅛ tsp. table salt
- 1 Tbsp. olive oil
- 1 Tbsp. all-purpose flour
- 1¼ cups reduced-sodium fat-free chicken broth
- ½ cup chopped green onions
- 2 garlic cloves, minced
- 1 Tbsp. fresh lemon juice
- ¼ tsp. table salt
- ¼ tsp. hot sauce
- 2 cups firmly packed fresh baby spinach

1. Prepare Parmesan Grits: Bring ½ tsp. salt and 4 cups water to a boil in a medium saucepan; gradually whisk in grits. Cook over medium heat, stirring occasionally, 8 minutes or until thickened. Whisk in cheese and black pepper. Keep warm.

2. Prepare Creamy Shrimp Sauce: Peel shrimp; devein, if desired. Sprinkle shrimp with black pepper and ⅛ tsp. salt. Cook in a large non-stick skillet coated with cooking spray over medium-high heat 1 to 2 minutes on each side or just until shrimp turn pink. Remove from skillet. Reduce heat to medium. Add oil; heat 30 seconds. Whisk in flour; cook 30 seconds to 1 minute. Whisk in broth and next 5 ingredients; cook 2 to 3 minutes or until thickened. Stir in shrimp and spinach; cook 1 minute or until spinach is slightly wilted. Serve immediately over grits.

grocery guide:

- ❏ 1 lb. unpeeled, medium-size raw shrimp
- ❏ 1 bunch green onions
- ❏ 1 small garlic bulb
- ❏ 1 lemon
- ❏ 1 (10-oz.) bag fresh baby spinach

Grilled Scallop Kabobs

**MAKES: 4 TO 6 SERVINGS   HANDS-ON TIME: 15 MIN.
TOTAL TIME: 15 MIN.**

20	fresh thick asparagus	¼	cup herb-flavored olive oil*
40	sea scallops (about 1 ½ lb.)		Lemon wedges
10	(6-inch) metal skewers		

1. Preheat grill to 350° to 400° (medium-high) heat. Snap off and discard tough ends of asparagus. Cut asparagus into 2-inch pieces. Thread scallops alternately with asparagus pieces onto each skewer. Brush with oil.

2. Grill kabobs, covered with grill lid, 2 ½ minutes on each side or just until scallops are opaque. Sprinkle with salt to taste. Serve kabobs with lemon wedges.

   * We tested with Benissimo Mediterranean Garlic Gourmet Oil.

Make It Gourmet:
Round out the meal with grilled pita wedges and deli tabbouleh salad.

grocery guide:

- ❏ 2 bunches thick asparagus
- ❏ 40 sea scallops (about 1 ½ lb.)
- ❏ 10 (6-inch) metal skewers
- ❏ 1 (8.1-oz.) bottle herb-flavored olive oil
- ❏ 1 lemon

Pesto Mussels with Parmesan Garlic Toasts

MAKES: 4 SERVINGS   **HANDS-ON TIME: 13 MIN.**
TOTAL TIME: 28 MIN.

For a fresher flavor, make your own pesto instead of buying the commercial variety.

1	(8.5-oz.) French bread baguette	¼	tsp. freshly ground black pepper
¼	cup garlic-and-herb butter, softened	2	lb. fresh mussels, scrubbed and debearded
¾	cup thinly sliced shallots (2 large)	¼	cup jarred refrigerated pesto
2	Tbsp. olive oil	¼	cup butter, softened
4	garlic cloves, thinly sliced	½	cup (2 oz.) finely shredded Parmesan cheese
1	cup dry white wine		
¼	tsp. kosher salt		

grocery guide:

- ❏ 1 (8.5-oz.) French bread baguette
- ❏ 1 (8-oz.) jar garlic-and-herb butter
- ❏ 1 package shallots
- ❏ 1 small garlic bulb
- ❏ 2 lb. fresh mussels

1. Preheat oven to 400°. Cut baguette in half crosswise; cut each piece in half horizontally. Spread cut sides of baguette with garlic-and-herb butter. Place bread on a baking sheet; bake at 400° for 8 minutes or until toasted.

2. Meanwhile, sauté shallots in hot oil in a large Dutch oven over medium-high heat 3 minutes or until tender. Add garlic; sauté 1 minute. Add wine, salt, and black pepper; bring to a boil over medium-high heat. Add mussels; cook, covered, 5 minutes or until mussels open. Remove from heat; discard any unopened shells.

3. Stir together pesto and softened butter; add to mussels, stirring until butter melts. Keep warm.

4. Preheat broiler with oven rack 5 ½ inches from heat. Place toasted bread on a lightly greased rack in a broiler pan. Sprinkle bread evenly with Parmesan cheese. Broil 1 minute or just until cheese melts. Serve toast with mussels and cooking liquid.

Crab Quesadillas

MAKES: 4 SERVINGS   **HANDS-ON TIME: 15 MIN.**
TOTAL TIME: 15 MIN.

Bursting with crab flavor, these irresistibly creamy quesadillas are ready in just minutes.

1	lb. fresh lump crabmeat, drained	2	Tbsp. chopped fresh cilantro
1	(3-oz.) package cream cheese, softened	2	Tbsp. sour cream
¼	cup chopped green onions	4	(8-inch) soft taco-size flour tortillas
¼	cup diced red bell pepper	1	cup (4 oz.) shredded Monterey Jack cheese
¼	cup frozen whole kernel corn, thawed		Garnish: lime wedges

1. Pick crabmeat, removing any bits of shell. Stir together cream cheese and next 5 ingredients in a medium bowl. Add crabmeat, stirring gently to coat.

2. Spoon about ¾ cup crab mixture over half of each tortilla; sprinkle cheese evenly over crab mixture. Fold tortillas in half, pressing gently to seal.

3. Place 2 quesadillas in a hot, lightly greased skillet or griddle over medium-high heat; cook 2 minutes on each side or until cheese melts and tortillas are lightly browned. Remove from skillet; keep warm. Repeat procedure with remaining quesadillas. Cut each quesadilla into wedges, if desired.

Kid Flip: Substitute 3 cups of cooked chicken for the crabmeat, if desired. One rotisserie chicken yields 3 cups.

grocery guide:

❑ 1 lb. fresh lump crabmeat
❑ 1 (3-oz.) package cream cheese
❑ 1 bunch green onions
❑ 1 red bell pepper
❑ 1 bunch cilantro
❑ Optional: 1 lime

Tomato-Basil Bisque

MAKES: ABOUT 7 CUPS   **HANDS-ON TIME: 15 MIN.**
TOTAL TIME: 15 MIN.

2	(10 ¾-oz.) cans tomato soup	¼	tsp. freshly ground black pepper
1	(14 ½-oz.) can diced tomatoes		Toppings: fresh basil leaves, freshly ground black pepper, shaved Parmesan cheese
2 ½	cups buttermilk		
2	Tbsp. chopped fresh basil		

grocery guide:
- ❏ 2 (10 ¾-oz.) cans tomato soup
- ❏ 1 qt. buttermilk
- ❏ 1 bunch fresh basil

Cook first 5 ingredients in a 3-qt. saucepan over medium heat, stirring often, 6 to 8 minutes or until thoroughly heated. Serve immediately with desired toppings.

Stretch Your Budget: Save time and money
by adding a few fresh ingredients to canned soup you already have on hand in your pantry.

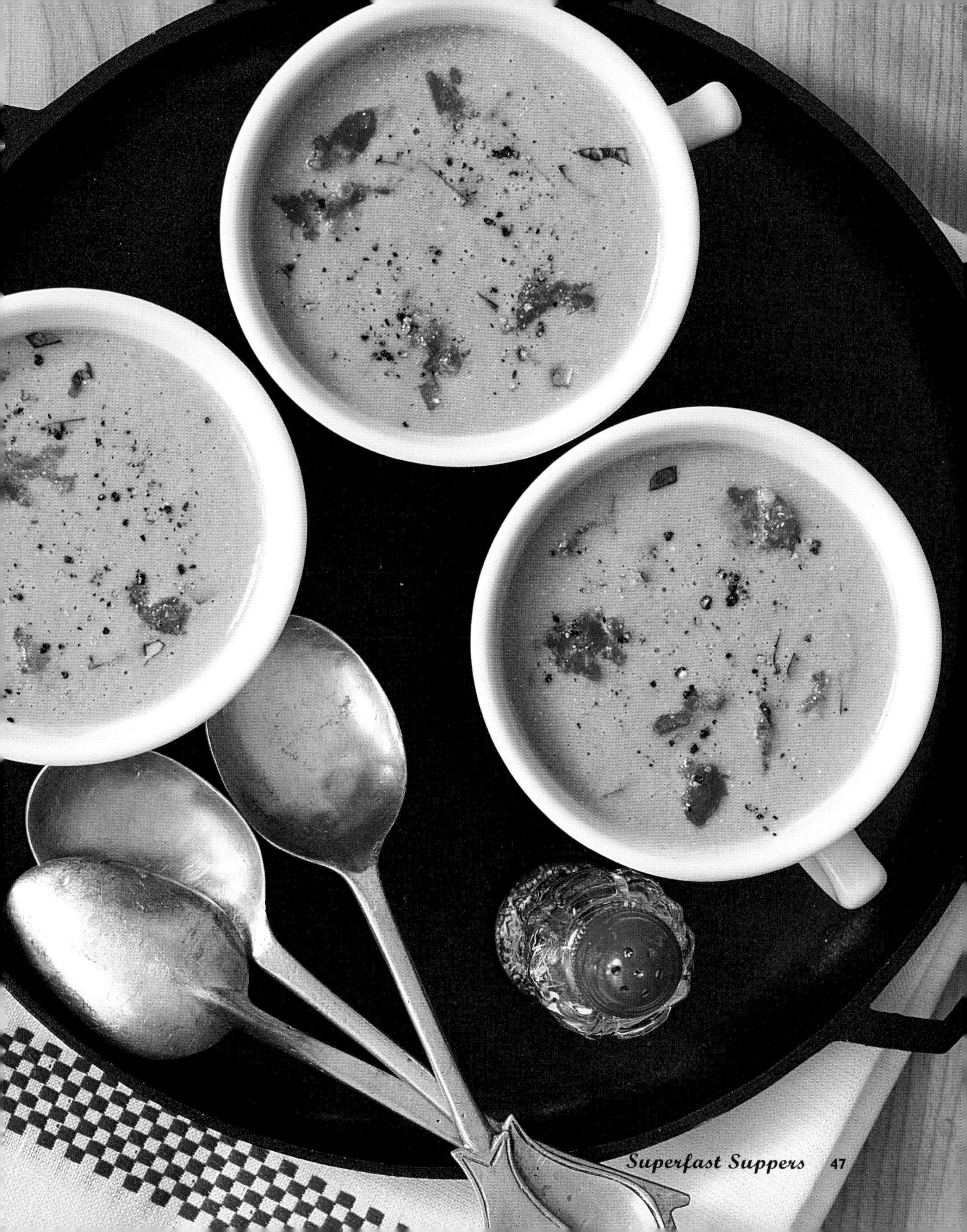

Fettuccine-and-Asparagus al Burro

**MAKES: 3 TO 4 SERVINGS HANDS-ON TIME: 30 MIN.
TOTAL TIME: 30 MIN.**

Al burro means "buttered." This simple sauce is a more authentic version of today's popular Alfredo, which calls for whipping cream. Buy a high-quality cheese—it makes a difference.

1   lb. fresh thin asparagus
4 to 6 oz. thick pancetta slices, diced
1   (9-oz.) package refrigerated fettuccine*
2   Tbsp. butter, at room temperature
3   Tbsp. extra virgin olive oil

½   cup freshly shredded Parmigiano-Reggiano cheese
2   Tbsp. chopped fresh flat-leaf parsley
¼   tsp. table salt
¼   tsp. freshly ground black pepper
Toppings: shaved Parmesan cheese, freshly ground black pepper

grocery guide:
❏ I bunch fresh thin asparagus
❏ 4 to 6 oz. thick pancetta slices
❏ I (9-oz.) package refrigerated fettuccine
❏ I oz. Parmigiano-Reggiano cheese
❏ I bunch fresh flat-leaf parsley

1. Snap off and discard tough ends of asparagus. Cut diagonally into 1½-inch pieces.

2. Sauté pancetta in a large skillet over medium heat 5 minutes or until crisp; remove from skillet.

3. Cook fettuccine and asparagus in boiling salted water to cover 2 to 3 minutes. Drain, reserving ¼ cup pasta water.

4. Melt butter with oil in skillet over medium heat; add hot cooked pasta and asparagus, cheese, and next 3 ingredients. Toss to coat, adding enough reserved pasta water to make a glossy sauce. Remove from heat; sprinkle with pancetta. Serve immediately with desired toppings.

*We tested with Buitoni All Natural Fettuccine.

Fettuccine with Zucchini and Pecans

MAKES: 6 SERVINGS **HANDS-ON TIME: 24 MIN.**
TOTAL TIME: 24 MIN.

1	(12-oz.) package fettuccine	¾	cup toasted coarsely chopped pecans
2	Tbsp. butter		
2	Tbsp. olive oil	1	cup freshly grated Asiago cheese
1	lb. small zucchini, shredded		
2	garlic cloves, minced	¼	cup small fresh basil leaves

1. Prepare fettuccine according to package directions.

2. Meanwhile, melt butter with oil in a large nonstick skillet over medium-high heat; add zucchini and garlic, and sauté 3 to 4 minutes or until zucchini is tender. Toss with hot cooked fettuccine, toasted pecans, Asiago cheese, and basil. Season with salt and freshly ground pepper to taste. Serve immediately.

grocery guide:

- ❏ 1 (12-oz.) package fettuccine
- ❏ 1 lb. small zucchini
- ❏ 1 small garlic bulb
- ❏ 4 oz. Asiago cheese
- ❏ 1 bunch fresh basil

soups, salads & sandwiches

Prepare homemade soups, sandwiches, and salads faster than you can pick up takeout.

Peach-and-Tomato Gazpacho with Cucumber Yogurt

MAKES: ABOUT 5 CUPS **HANDS-ON TIME: 20 MIN.**
TOTAL TIME: 1 HOUR, 20 MIN.

5   large peaches, peeled and divided
3   large tomatoes, cored and divided
½   medium-size sweet onion, coarsely chopped (about ½ cup)
3   Tbsp. apple cider vinegar
Kosher salt

Freshly ground white pepper
¾   cup finely diced English cucumber
⅓   cup plain Greek yogurt
2   Tbsp. chopped fresh chives
1   garlic clove, minced
Extra virgin olive oil
Garnish: fresh chives

1. Quarter 4 peaches and 2 tomatoes. Process quartered peaches and tomatoes and next 2 ingredients in a food processor until smooth.

2. Chop remaining peach and tomato. Stir into pureed mixture. Season with kosher salt and freshly ground white pepper to taste. Cover and chill 1 hour.

3. Meanwhile, combine cucumber and next 3 ingredients in a medium bowl. Season with kosher salt and freshly ground white pepper to taste. Cover and chill 1 to 24 hours. (Chilling can dull the seasoning, so you may need to add more salt and pepper before serving.)

4. Ladle gazpacho into bowls. Spoon cucumber mixture over gazpacho. Drizzle each serving with about 1 tsp. extra virgin olive oil. Serve immediately.

grocery guide:
- ❑ 5 large peaches
- ❑ 3 large tomatoes
- ❑ 1 medium-size sweet onion
- ❑ 1 English cucumber
- ❑ 1 (6-oz.) container Greek yogurt
- ❑ 1 (0.75-oz.) package fresh chives
- ❑ 1 small garlic bulb

Taco Soup

**MAKES: 14 CUPS HANDS-ON TIME: 20 MIN.
TOTAL TIME: 58 MIN.**

Taco Soup is the go-to recipe for an easy night of entertaining friends or a quick weeknight supper for your family. Most of the ingredients are pantry staples, so you'll be able to put together this recipe quickly.

- 1 lb. ground beef
- 2 (16-oz.) cans pinto beans, drained and rinsed
- 1 (16-oz.) package frozen cut green beans
- 1 (15-oz.) can ranch beans, undrained
- 1 (14.5-oz.) can stewed tomatoes
- 1 (14.5-oz.) can petite diced tomatoes, undrained
- 1 (12-oz.) package frozen whole kernel corn
- 1 (12-oz.) bottle beer
- 1 (1-oz.) envelope taco seasoning mix
- 1 (1-oz.) envelope Ranch dressing mix

Toppings: corn chips, shredded Cheddar cheese

1. Brown ground beef in a large Dutch oven over medium-high heat, stirring constantly, 5 minutes or until meat crumbles and is no longer pink; drain. Return to Dutch oven.

2. Stir pinto beans, next 8 ingredients, and 2 cups water into beef; bring to a boil. Reduce heat to medium-low. Simmer, stirring occasionally, 30 minutes. Serve with desired toppings.

The Sandwich: Sprinkle shredded pepper Jack cheese on 6 (6-inch) fajita-size flour tortillas. Fold tortillas in half, press gently to seal, and spread butter on each. Cook quesadillas in a hot skillet 2 to 3 minutes on each side until browned. Cut into wedges.

Kid Flip: Substitute 1½ cups chicken broth for the bottle of beer.

grocery guide:

- ❏ 1 lb. ground beef
- ❏ 1 (16-oz.) package frozen cut green beans
- ❏ 1 (15-oz.) can ranch beans
- ❏ 1 (14.5-oz.) can stewed tomatoes
- ❏ 1 (12-oz.) bottle beer
- ❏ 1 (1 oz.) envelope Ranch dressing mix
- ❏ Optional: 1 (16-oz.) package corn chips

BLT Salad

MAKES: 4 SERVINGS   **HANDS-ON TIME: 30 MIN.**
TOTAL TIME: 40 MIN.

6	artisan bread slices, halved
2	Tbsp. extra virgin olive oil
1	tsp. kosher salt, divided
1	tsp. freshly ground black pepper, divided
6	thick applewood-smoked bacon slices, chopped
1	sweet onion, halved and sliced
1	garlic clove
½	cup mayonnaise
2	Tbsp. fresh lemon juice
1	lb. assorted heirloom tomatoes, cut into wedges
1	(5-oz.) package arugula

grocery guide:

❑ 1 loaf artisan bread
❑ 1 (12-oz.) package applewood-smoked bacon slices
❑ 1 sweet onion
❑ 1 small garlic bulb
❑ 1 lemon
❑ 1 lb. assorted heirloom tomatoes
❑ 1 (5-oz.) package arugula

1. Preheat oven to 400°. Drizzle bread with oil; sprinkle with ½ tsp. each kosher salt and black pepper. Bake bread in a single layer in a jelly-roll pan 12 minutes or until golden.

2. Cook bacon in a skillet over medium heat, stirring occasionally, 10 minutes or until crisp. Drain on paper towels; reserve 1 Tbsp. drippings in skillet.

3. Sauté onion in hot drippings over medium-low heat 3 to 5 minutes or until tender.

4. Smash garlic to make a paste. Whisk together mayonnaise, lemon juice, garlic paste, and remaining ½ tsp. each salt and black pepper.

5. Toss together tomatoes, arugula, bacon, and onion in a large bowl. Add additional salt and pepper to taste. Pour mayonnaise mixture over tomato mixture, and toss to coat. Serve immediately with toasted bread.

Asian Beef Salad

MAKES: 8 servings **HANDS-ON TIME: 30 min.**
TOTAL TIME: 1 hour, 30 min.

¼ cup teriyaki sauce
2 Tbsp. olive oil
2 (1-lb.) flank steaks
1 head napa cabbage, chopped
1 large head romaine lettuce, chopped
2 large tomatoes, cut into wedges
2 small cucumbers, thinly sliced
½ small red onion, thinly sliced
½ cup loosely packed fresh cilantro
Soy-Sesame Dressing

1. Combine teriyaki sauce and oil in a shallow dish or large zip-top plastic freezer bag; add steaks, turning to coat. Cover or seal, and chill 1 hour, turning steaks occasionally.

2. Remove steaks from marinade, discarding marinade.

3. Preheat grill to 350° to 400° (medium-high heat). Grill steaks, covered with grill lid, for 5 to 7 minutes on each side or to desired degree of doneness. Let stand 5 minutes; cut diagonally across the grain into thin strips.

4. Toss together steak slices, cabbage, and next 5 ingredients; drizzle with desired amount of dressing, tossing gently to coat.

Vanessa's Savvy Secret: No grill available? Cook the beef in a grill skillet on the cooktop.

grocery guide:

❏ 2 (1-lb.) flank steaks
❏ 1 head napa cabbage
❏ 1 large head romaine lettuce
❏ 2 large tomatoes
❏ 2 small cucumbers
❏ 1 small red onion
❏ 1 bunch fresh cilantro

Soy-Sesame Dressing

MAKES: ¾ CUP   **HANDS-ON TIME: 5 MIN.**
TOTAL TIME: 5 MIN.

Sesame oil lends a nutty flavor. Use the higher amount of Asian chili-garlic sauce for a spicier dressing. Refrigerate dressing in an airtight container up to 1 week.

¼	cup fresh lime juice	3	Tbsp. sesame oil
1	Tbsp. light brown sugar	2	Tbsp. lite soy sauce
3	Tbsp. olive oil	1 to 2 tsp. Asian chili-garlic sauce

Whisk together all ingredients.

grocery guide:

❑ 3 limes
❑ 1 (8-oz.) jar Asian chili-garlic sauce

Shrimp-Boil Potato Salad

MAKES: 6 SERVINGS   **HANDS-ON TIME: 30 MIN.**
TOTAL TIME: 30 MIN.

1 (3-oz.) package boil-in-bag shrimp-and-crab boil	½ cup fresh lemon juice
3 lb. baby red potatoes, halved	⅓ cup olive oil
1 lb. smoked link sausage, cut into ½-inch pieces*	¼ cup chopped fresh flat-leaf parsley
4 ears fresh corn, husks removed	3 Tbsp. Creole mustard
2 lb. peeled and deveined jumbo raw shrimp with tails	4 green onions, sliced
	1 garlic clove, pressed
	1 tsp. paprika
	1 tsp. refrigerated horseradish

1. Bring 10 cups water to a boil in a Dutch oven over high heat; add shrimp-and-crab boil, potatoes, and sausage; return to a boil, and cook 10 minutes. Add corn, and return to a boil. Cook 3 minutes or until potatoes are tender. Add shrimp; cover, remove from heat, and let stand 5 minutes or just until shrimp turn pink.

2. Meanwhile, whisk together lemon juice and next 7 ingredients in a medium bowl.

3. Drain shrimp mixture. Cut kernels from cobs. Discard cobs. Stir together corn kernels, shrimp mixture, and lemon juice mixture in a large bowl. Serve immediately, or cover and chill up to 24 hours.

  * We tested with Conecuh Original Smoked Sausage.

grocery guide:

- ❏ 1 (3-oz.) package boil-in-bag shrimp-and-crab boil
- ❏ 3 lb. baby red potatoes
- ❏ 1 lb. smoked link sausage
- ❏ 4 ears fresh corn
- ❏ 2 lb. peeled and deveined jumbo raw shrimp with tails
- ❏ 3 lemons
- ❏ 1 bunch fresh flat-leaf parsley
- ❏ 1 (5.25-oz.) jar Creole mustard
- ❏ 1 bunch green onions
- ❏ 1 small garlic bulb
- ❏ 1 (6.5-oz.) jar refrigerated horseradish

Ham Salad

MAKES: ABOUT 6 CUPS   **HANDS-ON TIME: 20 MIN.**
TOTAL TIME: 20 MIN.

2 lb. fully cooked boneless ham, cut into large chunks	1 tsp. fresh lemon juice
1 cup sweet pickle relish	¼ tsp. seasoned pepper
1 cup mayonnaise	3 to 5 hard-cooked eggs, peeled and chopped
1 Tbsp. celery seeds	Toasted French bread slices (optional)
1½ tsp. yellow mustard	
1 tsp. refrigerated horseradish	Garnish: chopped fresh parsley

Process ham, in batches, in a food processor until coarsely ground, stopping to scrape down sides as needed. Place ground ham in a bowl; stir in pickle relish and next 6 ingredients. Fold in chopped eggs. Serve on toasted bread slices.

Kid Flip:
Classic ham salad gets a new look atop toasted crostini, but it's just as delicious sandwiched between two slices of bread.

grocery guide:

- ☐ 2 lb. fully cooked boneless ham
- ☐ 1 (12.7-oz.) bottle sweet pickle relish
- ☐ 1 (0.95-oz.) jar celery seeds
- ☐ 1 (6.5-oz.) jar refrigerated horseradish
- ☐ 1 lemon
- ☐ 1 loaf French bread
- ☐ Optional: 1 bunch fresh parsley

Warm Frisée Salad with Crispy Kosher Salami

MAKES: 8 SERVINGS   **HANDS-ON TIME: 25 MIN.**
TOTAL TIME: 25 MIN.

Frisée is a member of the chicory family often used in mesclun salad mixes. Buy bunches with crisp leaves and no signs of wilting. Use all the leaves except the core.

½	(12-oz.) package kosher beef salami slices*	2	tsp. whole grain mustard
¼	cup extra virgin olive oil	½	tsp. kosher salt
½	medium-size red onion, sliced	¼	tsp. coarsely ground black pepper
1	garlic clove, minced	4	bunches frisée, torn**
⅓	cup plus 1 Tbsp. sherry vinegar	1	pt. grape tomatoes, halved

1. Cut kosher beef salami slices into ¼-inch strips.

2. Cook salami strips in hot olive oil in a medium skillet over medium heat 5 to 10 minutes or until crispy. Remove salami with a slotted spoon, reserving remaining oil in skillet. Drain salami pieces on paper towels.

3. Sauté onion and garlic in reserved hot oil 2 minutes. Stir in vinegar, mustard, salt, and black pepper; cook 1 minute.

4. Place frisée and grape tomato halves in a large bowl, and drizzle with vinegar mixture; toss to coat. Sprinkle with crispy salami pieces, and serve immediately.

* We tested with Hebrew National Kosher Beef Salami.

** 2 bunches curly endive leaves may be substituted.

grocery guide:

- ❏ 1 (12-oz.) package kosher beef salami slices
- ❏ 1 medium-size red onion
- ❏ 1 small garlic bulb
- ❏ 4 bunches frisée
- ❏ 1 pt. grape tomatoes

Slaw Reubens

MAKES: 2 servings **HANDS-ON TIME: 14 MIN.**
TOTAL TIME: 14 MIN.

2   cups shredded coleslaw mix
5   Tbsp. Thousand Island
     dressing, divided
1   Tbsp. white vinegar
¼   tsp. freshly ground black
     pepper
1   tsp. spicy brown mustard
4   rye or pumpernickel bread
     slices

1   (7-oz.) package shaved
     roast beef
½   Granny Smith apple, cored
     and thinly sliced
2   (1-oz.) Swiss cheese slices
2   Tbsp. butter, melted

1. Stir together coleslaw mix, 2 Tbsp. dressing, vinegar, and black pepper in a medium bowl.

2. Stir together spicy brown mustard and remaining 3 Tbsp. dressing; spread dressing mixture evenly on 1 side of bread slices. Top 2 bread slices evenly with beef, half of apple slices, and 1 cheese slice. Divide slaw mixture evenly over cheese. Top with remaining bread slices, dressing mixture sides down. Brush both sides of sandwiches evenly with melted butter.

3. Cook sandwiches in a large lightly greased nonstick skillet over medium-high heat 2 minutes on each side or until golden. Serve immediately.

grocery guide:

❏ 1 (16-oz.) package shredded
   coleslaw mix
❏ 1 loaf rye or pumpernickel
   bread
❏ 1 (7-oz.) package shaved
   roast beef
❏ 1 Granny Smith apple
❏ 1 (8-oz.) package Swiss cheese
   slices

Roasted Vegetable Sandwiches

MAKES: 4 SERVINGS   HANDS-ON TIME: 20 MIN.
TOTAL TIME: 30 MIN., NOT INCLUDING VEGETABLES

¼	cup butter, softened	4	tsp. mayonnaise
1	garlic clove, pressed	3	cups Roasted Summer
¼	tsp. dried Italian seasoning		Vegetables
4	French hamburger buns, split*	4	provolone cheese slices

1. Preheat oven to 400°.

2. Stir together first 3 ingredients.

3. Spread butter mixture on cut sides of top bun halves; spread mayonnaise on cut sides of bottom bun halves. Layer bottom bun halves, mayonnaise sides up, with ¾ cup Roasted Summer Vegetables and cheese. Top with remaining bun halves. Wrap each sandwich lightly in aluminum foil, and place on a baking sheet.

4. Bake at 400° for 10 to 12 minutes or until cheese melts.

* We tested with Publix Deli French Hamburger Buns.

grocery guide:

- ❏ 1 small garlic bulb
- ❏ 1 (8-count) package French hamburger buns
- ❏ 1 (8-oz.) package provolone cheese slices

Roasted Summer Vegetables

MAKES: 6 TO 8 SERVINGS   HANDS-ON TIME: 30 MIN.
TOTAL TIME: 1 HOUR, 10 MIN.

1	medium eggplant	3	Tbsp. olive oil
1	tsp. table salt, divided	½	tsp. black pepper
2	medium zucchini (about 1 lb.)	3	Tbsp. chopped fresh basil
3	yellow squash (about 1¼ lb.)	1	Tbsp. chopped fresh parsley
1	red bell pepper		
1	medium-size red onion, halved		

1. Preheat oven to 450°.

2. Cut eggplant into ¼-inch-thick slices, and place in a single layer on paper towels. Sprinkle with ½ tsp. salt, and let stand 20 minutes.

3. Cut zucchini and yellow squash into ¼-inch-thick slices. Cut bell pepper into ½-inch strips. Cut onion halves into ½-inch-thick slices.

4. Toss together vegetables, oil, remaining ½ tsp. salt, and black pepper; place on 3 lightly greased broiler pans or jelly-roll pans.

5. Bake at 450° for 20 minutes or until tender, stirring once. Remove from oven, and sprinkle with basil and parsley.

grocery guide:

- ❏ 1 medium eggplant
- ❏ 2 medium zucchini
- ❏ 3 yellow squash
- ❏ 1 red bell pepper
- ❏ 1 medium-size red onion
- ❏ 1 bunch fresh basil
- ❏ 1 bunch fresh parsley

Chicken Salad with Grapes and Pecans

MAKES: 4 SERVINGS   **HANDS-ON TIME: 20 MIN.**
TOTAL TIME: 1 HOUR, 20 MIN.

½	cup light or regular mayonnaise	2	lb. skinned and boned chicken breasts, cooked and chopped
½	cup reduced-fat or regular sour cream	3	cups red and white seedless grapes, halved
1	Tbsp. fresh lemon juice	1	cup toasted chopped pecans
1	tsp. table salt		Lettuce leaves (optional)
½	tsp. black pepper		

Stir together ½ cup mayonnaise and next 4 ingredients in a large bowl. Add chopped chicken and grapes, tossing gently to coat. Cover and chill at least 1 hour. Stir in pecans just before serving. Serve in stemware lined with lettuce leaves, if desired.

Gourmet Flip: Serve this fruity, nutty chicken salad with assorted crackers and grapes for a filling lunch or a delicious brunch.

grocery guide:

❏ 1 lemon
❏ 2 lb. skinned and boned chicken breasts
❏ 1 lb. red and white seedless grapes
❏ Optional: 1 head green leaf lettuce

Miss Mattie's Southern Pimiento Cheese

MAKES: ABOUT 5 CUPS   **HANDS-ON TIME: 30 MIN.**
TOTAL TIME: 30 MIN.

- 1 cup mayonnaise
- 1 (7-oz.) jar diced pimientos, drained
- ½ cup chopped sweet-hot pickled jalapeño pepper slices*
- 1 Tbsp. liquid from sweet-hot jalapeño pepper slices
- ½ cup toasted chopped pecans
- 4 cups (1 lb.) freshly grated mild Cheddar cheese

Garnish: sweet-hot pickled jalapeño pepper slices

1. Stir together mayonnaise and next 4 ingredients.
2. Stir in Cheddar cheese until well blended.

   * We tested with The Original Texas Sweet & Hot Jalapeños.

grocery guide:

❏ 1 (6-oz.) jar sweet-hot pickled jalapeño pepper slices
❏ 1 (16-oz.) block Cheddar cheese

Country Ham-and-Peach Panini

MAKES: 4 SERVINGS　　**HANDS-ON TIME: 20 MIN.**
TOTAL TIME: 20 MIN.

8	ciabatta bread slices*	4	oz. thinly sliced country ham,
4	tsp. coarse-grained Dijon		prosciutto, or serrano ham
	mustard	2	medium peaches (about
	Freshly ground black pepper		¾ lb.), unpeeled and sliced
4	(1-oz.) fontina cheese	4	tsp. honey (optional)
	slices	1	Tbsp. extra virgin olive oil

1. Spread each of 4 bread slices with 1 tsp. mustard, and sprinkle with desired amount of freshly ground pepper. Layer with cheese, ham, peaches, and, if desired, honey. Top with remaining bread slices, and press together gently. Brush sandwiches with oil.

2. Cook sandwiches, in batches, in a preheated panini press 3 to 4 minutes or until golden brown and cheese is melted. (Or use a preheated nonstick grill pan, and cook sandwiches over medium heat 3 to 4 minutes on each side.) Serve immediately.

　* Any firm white bread may be substituted.

Vanessa's Savvy Secret: It's best to use very thinly sliced ham, not thick ham steaks. Ask your deli to slice it, or look for a packet of center- and end-cut slices, which tend to be smaller.

grocery guide:
- ❑ 1 ciabatta bread loaf, sliced
- ❑ 1 (8-oz.) package fontina cheese slices
- ❑ 4 oz. thinly sliced country ham, prosciutto, or serrano ham
- ❑ 2 medium peaches

Fried Green Tomato Sliders

MAKES: 12 SERVINGS **HANDS-ON TIME: 20 MIN.**
TOTAL TIME: 30 MIN.

1½ cups shredded red cabbage	½ cup mayonnaise
1½ cups shredded napa cabbage	2 to 3 tsp. Asian hot chili sauce
¼ cup matchstick carrots	(such as Sriracha)
⅓ cup thinly sliced red onion	12 slider buns or dinner rolls,
3 Tbsp. olive oil	warmed and split
2 Tbsp. fresh lime juice	12 cooked bacon slices
½ cup chopped fresh cilantro,	12 Fried Green Tomatoes
divided	

1. Stir together first 6 ingredients and ¼ cup cilantro in a medium bowl. Season with salt and pepper to taste. Let stand 10 minutes.

2. Stir together mayonnaise, chili sauce, and remaining ¼ cup cilantro. Spread buns with mayonnaise mixture. Top bottom halves of buns with bacon, tomatoes, and cabbage mixture. Cover with top halves of buns, mayonnaise mixture sides down.

Make It Snappy:
Start with fried green tomatoes from your favorite meat 'n' three restaurant instead of making your own. Bake them on a baking sheet at 350° for 5 minutes or until warm and crispy.

grocery guide:

- ❏ 1 head red cabbage
- ❏ 1 head napa cabbage
- ❏ 1 small red onion
- ❏ 2 limes
- ❏ 1 bunch fresh cilantro
- ❏ 12 slider buns or dinner rolls
- ❏ 1 (16-oz.) package matchstick carrots

Fried Green Tomatoes

MAKES: 4 TO 6 SERVINGS   **HANDS-ON TIME: 10 MIN.**
TOTAL TIME: 10 MIN.

1	large egg, lightly beaten	½	tsp. black pepper
½	cup buttermilk	3	medium-size green tomatoes,
½	cup all-purpose flour, divided		cut into ⅓-inch slices
½	cup cornmeal		Vegetable oil
1	tsp. table salt		

1. Stir together egg and buttermilk in a small bowl; set aside.

2. Stir together ¼ cup flour and next 3 ingredients in a shallow bowl or pan.

3. Dredge tomato slices in remaining ¼ cup flour; dip in egg mixture, shaking off excess, and dredge in cornmeal mixture.

4. Pour oil to depth of ¼ to ½ inch in a large heavy skillet; heat to 375°. Drop tomatoes, in batches, into hot oil, and cook 2 minutes on each side or until golden. Drain on paper towels or a rack over paper towels. Sprinkle hot tomatoes with salt to taste.

grocery guide:
❏ 1 pt. buttermilk
❏ 3 medium-size green tomatoes

Ham-and-Fontina Sourdough Sandwiches

MAKES: 4 servings **HANDS-ON TIME: 10 min.**
TOTAL TIME: 10 min.

It's what's inside that counts here. Deli ham gets dressed up with good stuff like a pesto-mayonnaise spread, fontina cheese, and basil leaves.

½ cup mayonnaise
3 Tbsp. jarred refrigerated pesto sauce
1 tsp. fresh lemon juice
8 sourdough bakery bread slices
16 fontina cheese slices (about ½ lb.)
1 large red bell pepper, cut into thin strips
16 thin deli ham slices (about ½ lb.)
12 fresh basil leaves
8 Bibb lettuce leaves

1. Stir together first 3 ingredients.

2. Spread I side of each bread slice generously with mayonnaise mixture. Layer cheese, bell pepper strips, ham, basil, and lettuce on half of bread slices. Top with remaining bread slices, mayonnaise mixture sides down. Cut sandwiches in half.

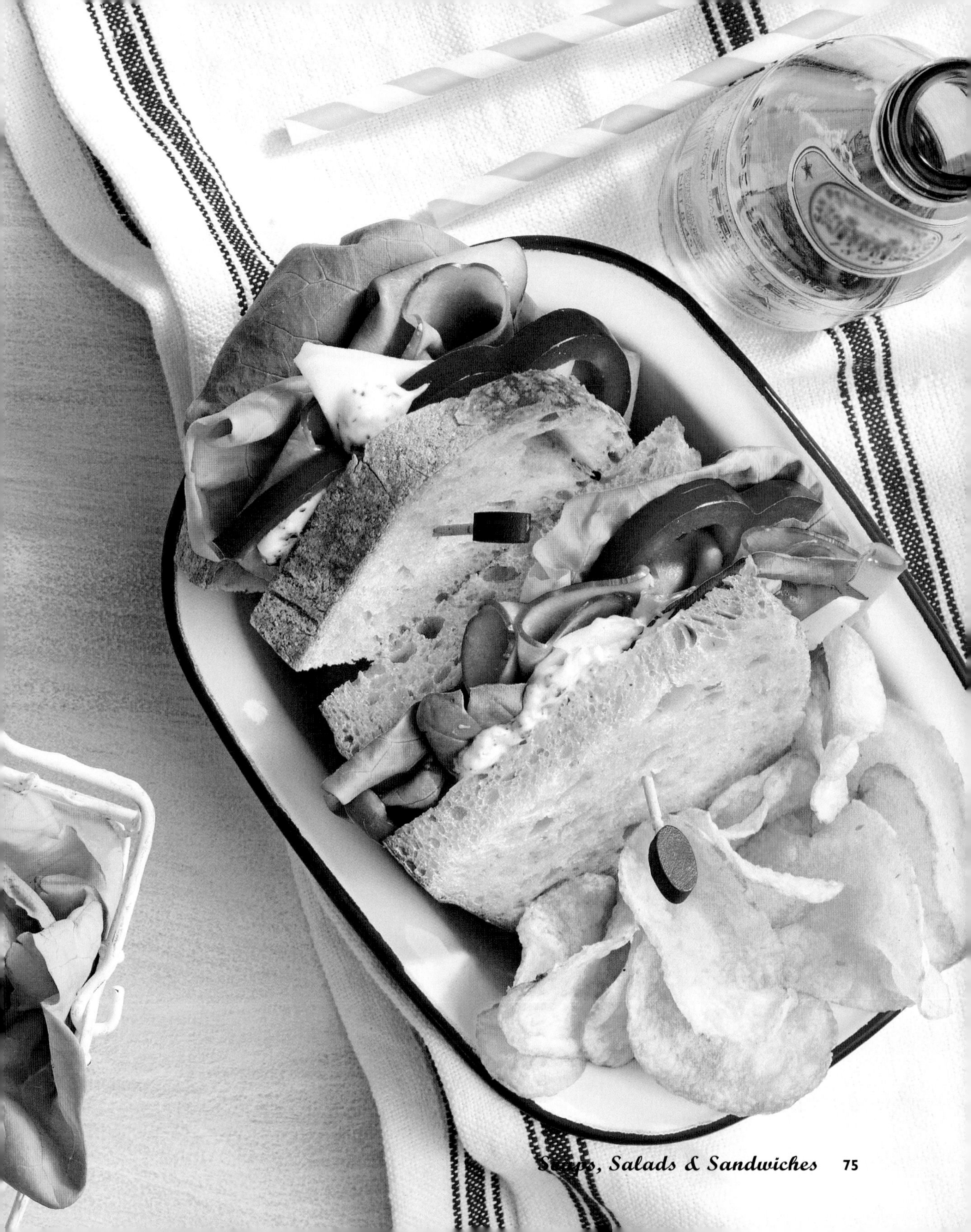

Beef-and-Arugula Ciabatta Sandwiches

MAKES: 8 servings   **HANDS-ON TIME: 10 min.**
TOTAL TIME: 25 min.

Any way you slice them, Beef-and-Arugula Ciabatta Sandwiches give you a bit of everything in each bite. These sandwiches get their zing from the red pepper jelly that's stirred into the mayonnaise.

½	cup mayonnaise	8	rare deli roast beef slices (about ½ lb.)
3	Tbsp. red pepper jelly	8	Havarti cheese slices (about ½ lb.)
1	(12-oz.) package frozen individual ciabatta rolls	2	cups loosely packed arugula

1. Preheat oven to 400°. Whisk together first 2 ingredients.

2. Place rolls on a baking sheet. Bake at 400° for 5 minutes or until lightly toasted but still soft. Let cool 10 minutes; split rolls.

3. Spread cut sides of rolls with mayonnaise mixture. Layer bottom roll halves with beef, folding slices as needed to fit rolls. Top each with cheese, arugula, and remaining roll halves, mayonnaise mixture sides down.

grocery guide:

- ❏ 1 (10.5-oz.) jar red pepper jelly
- ❏ 1 (12-oz.) package frozen individual ciabatta rolls
- ❏ 8 rare deli roast beef slices (about ½ lb.)
- ❏ 8 Havarti cheese slices (about ½ lb.)
- ❏ 1 (5-oz.) package arugula

Pancetta-Arugula-Turkey Sandwiches

MAKES: 6 SERVINGS   **HANDS-ON TIME: 15 MIN.**
TOTAL TIME: 15 MIN.

12	multigrain sourdough bakery bread slices	12	cooked pancetta slices
5	oz. soft-ripened blue cheese*	2	cups loosely packed arugula
1½	lb. sliced roasted turkey	¼	cup whole grain Dijon mustard
½	cup whole-berry cranberry sauce		

Spread 1 side of 6 bread slices with blue cheese. Layer with turkey, cranberry sauce, pancetta, and arugula. Spread 1 side of remaining 6 bread slices with mustard, and place, mustard sides down, on arugula.

  * We tested with Saga Classic Soft-Ripened Blue-Veined Cheese.

grocery guide:

- ❏ 1 multigrain sourdough bakery bread loaf, sliced
- ❏ 5 oz. soft-ripened blue cheese
- ❏ 1½ lb. sliced roasted turkey
- ❏ 1 (14-oz.) can whole-berry cranberry sauce
- ❏ 12 pancetta slices
- ❏ 1 (5-oz.) package arugula

company's coming

Having friends over during
a busy week can be a
relaxing break with these dishes.

Pan-Seared Skirt Steaks

MAKES: 8 SERVINGS   **HANDS-ON TIME: 25 MIN.**
TOTAL TIME: 55 MIN., INCLUDING CHILL TIME

1 jalapeño pepper	1¼ tsp. kosher salt
½ cup dry red wine	1 tsp. freshly ground black
3 Tbsp. Worcestershire sauce	pepper
1 cup chopped fresh cilantro,	3 Tbsp. fresh lime juice
divided	Additional kosher salt
3 Tbsp. olive oil, divided	Additional freshly ground black
2 garlic cloves, minced and	pepper
divided	Sweet Potato Hash
2 (1-lb.) skirt steaks	

1. Halve, seed, and mince jalapeño pepper. Combine red wine, Worcestershire sauce, ¼ cup chopped fresh cilantro, 1 Tbsp. olive oil, half of jalapeño pepper, and 1 minced garlic clove in a large zip-top plastic freezer bag. Add steak; seal and chill 30 minutes to 24 hours. (If marinating overnight, let steak stand in marinade at room temperature 30 minutes.)

2. Remove from marinade, discarding marinade. Sprinkle steak with 1¼ tsp. kosher salt and 1 tsp. freshly ground black pepper.

3. Heat a grill pan over medium-high heat. Cook steaks, in batches, 2 minutes on each side (medium-rare) or to desired degree of doneness. Remove from grill pan, cover loosely with aluminum foil, and let stand 5 minutes.

4. Stir together remaining ¾ cup chopped fresh cilantro, lime juice, remaining 2 Tbsp. olive oil, remaining 1 minced garlic clove, and remaining half of jalapeño pepper. Season with kosher salt and freshly ground pepper to taste. Cut steaks diagonally across the grain into thin slices. Serve with cilantro sauce and Sweet Potato Hash.

grocery guide:
❑ 1 jalapeño pepper
❑ 1 bunch fresh cilantro
❑ 1 small garlic bulb
❑ 2 (1-lb.) skirt steaks
❑ 3 limes

Sweet Potato Hash

MAKES: 8 SERVINGS **HANDS-ON TIME: 15 MIN.**
TOTAL TIME: 15 MIN.

1	Tbsp. butter	½	red onion, chopped
2	Tbsp. olive oil	1	tsp. kosher salt
2	sweet potatoes, peeled and chopped	¼	teaspoon freshly ground black pepper
½	red bell pepper, chopped		

Melt butter with oil in a skillet over medium-high heat. Add sweet potatoes; cook, stirring occasionally, 5 minutes. Add bell pepper, onion, kosher salt, and freshly ground pepper. Reduce heat to medium; cover and cook, stirring occasionally, 8 to 10 minutes or until potatoes are tender.

grocery guide:

❑ 2 sweet potatoes
❑ 1 red bell pepper
❑ 1 small red onion

Beef-and-Brussels Sprouts Stir-fry

MAKES: 4 SERVINGS   **HANDS-ON TIME: 20 MIN.**
TOTAL TIME: 20 MIN.

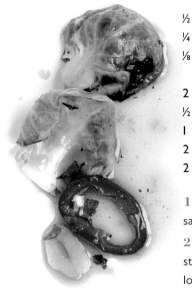

½	lb. flank steak
¼	tsp. table salt
⅛	tsp. freshly ground black pepper
2	Tbsp. peanut oil, divided
½	cup beef broth or water
1	Tbsp. light brown sugar
2	Tbsp. soy sauce
2	tsp. fresh lime juice
½	tsp. cornstarch
12	oz. fresh Brussels sprouts, trimmed and halved
1	red jalapeño or red serrano pepper, sliced
1	Tbsp. grated fresh ginger
2	garlic cloves, thinly sliced
¼	cup chopped fresh mint
	Hot cooked rice

1. Cut steak diagonally across the grain into thin strips. Sprinkle with salt and pepper.

2. Stir-fry steak, in 2 batches, in 1 Tbsp. hot oil in a large cast-iron or stainless-steel skillet over high heat 2 to 3 minutes or until meat is no longer pink. Transfer steak to a plate, and wipe skillet clean.

3. Whisk together beef broth and next 4 ingredients in a small bowl until smooth.

4. Stir-fry Brussels sprouts in remaining 1 Tbsp. hot oil over high heat 2 minutes or until lightly browned. Add jalapeño pepper, ginger, and garlic, and stir-fry 1 minute. Pour soy sauce mixture over Brussels sprouts, and bring mixture to a boil. Cook, stirring often, 3 to 4 minutes or until sprouts are tender. Stir in mint and steak. Serve over rice.

Kid Flip: Feel free to substitute any cruciferous vegetable cut into even pieces in place of Brussels sprouts, from broccoli and cauliflower to cabbage and bok choy.

grocery guide:

- ❑ ½ lb. flank steak
- ❑ 1 lime
- ❑ 12 oz. fresh Brussels sprouts
- ❑ 1 red jalapeño or red serrano pepper
- ❑ Fresh ginger
- ❑ 1 bunch fresh mint

Pimiento Cheese-Stuffed Burgers

MAKES: 4 SERVINGS   **HANDS-ON TIME: 32 MIN.**
TOTAL TIME: 1 HOUR, 2 MIN.

2	lb. ground chuck	4	hamburger buns
1	tsp. freshly ground black pepper	Toppings: tomato slices, red onion slices, lettuce leaves, mustard, mayonnaise, ketchup	
1 ⅓	cups prepared pimiento cheese, divided		
1	tsp. table salt		

1. Preheat grill to 350° to 400° (medium-high) heat. Combine ground beef and pepper in a large bowl until blended. (Do not overwork meat mixture.) Shape mixture into 8 (4-inch) patties; spoon 1½ Tbsp. pimiento cheese evenly into center of each of 4 patties. Top with remaining 4 patties, pressing edges to seal. Cover and chill 30 minutes. Sprinkle with salt.

2. Grill patties, covered with grill lid, 7 to 8 minutes on each side or until center is no longer pink. Serve on buns with desired toppings and remaining pimiento cheese.

grocery guide:

- ❑ 2 lb. ground chuck
- ❑ 1 (12-oz.) container prepared pimiento cheese
- ❑ 4 hamburger buns
- ❑ Optional: 1 tomato, 1 red onion, 1 head green leaf lettuce

Italian Meatballs

MAKES: 37 MEATBALLS **HANDS-ON TIME: 30 MIN.**
TOTAL TIME: 30 MIN.

2	lb. ground beef	2	large eggs, lightly beaten
1	cup Italian-seasoned breadcrumbs	½	tsp. table salt
1	cup freshly grated Parmesan cheese	¼	tsp. fennel seeds
1	cup chopped fresh flat-leaf parsley	¼	tsp. black pepper
		4	(10-inch) metal skewers
		Bottled barbecue sauce	
		Sandwich buns (optional)	

Combine ground beef and next 7 ingredients in a large bowl until blended. Shape into 37 (1½-inch) balls. Freeze up to 1 month. When ready to use, let stand at room temperature 10 minutes. Preheat grill to 350° to 400° (medium-high) heat. Thread meatballs onto skewers leaving a ⅛-inch space between pieces. Grill, covered with grill lid, 3 to 4 minutes on each side or until centers are no longer pink, basting with barbecue sauce during last 3 minutes. Serve on skewers.

Kid Flip: Serve these flavorful meatballs on sandwich buns with chips and fruit for a delicious weeknight meal.

grocery guide:

- ❏ 2 lb. ground beef
- ❏ 1 bunch fresh flat-leaf parsley
- ❏ 1 (1.5-oz.) jar fennel seeds
- ❏ 4 (10-inch) metal skewers
- ❏ Optional: sandwich buns

Taco Salad

MAKES: 6 SERVINGS   **HANDS-ON TIME: 25 MIN.**
TOTAL TIME: 25 MIN.

1 ½ lb. lean ground beef
1   (16-oz.) jar medium salsa
1   (16-oz.) can kidney beans,
     drained and rinsed
2   Tbsp. taco seasoning mix
2   avocados
½   cup sour cream

2   Tbsp. fresh cilantro
Bite-size tortilla chips
3   cups shredded lettuce
     (about ½ head)
Toppings: chopped tomato,
     finely chopped red onion,
     shredded cheese

1. Brown ground beef in a large nonstick skillet over medium-high heat, stirring often, 5 to 8 minutes until meat crumbles and is no longer pink. Drain and return to skillet. Stir in salsa, beans, and taco seasoning; bring to a boil. Reduce heat, and simmer, stirring occasionally, 10 minutes.

2. Peel and mash avocados; stir in sour cream and cilantro.

3. Place desired amount of tortilla chips on a serving platter, and top with shredded lettuce and beef mixture. Serve with avocado mixture and desired toppings.

grocery guide:

- ❑ 1 ½ lb. lean ground beef
- ❑ 1 (16-oz.) can kidney beans
- ❑ 2 avocados
- ❑ 1 bunch fresh cilantro
- ❑ Bite-size tortilla chips
- ❑ 1 head iceberg lettuce
- ❑ Optional: 1 tomato,
     1 red onion

Peach and Pork Kabobs

MAKES: 4 SERVINGS **HANDS-ON TIME: 30 MIN.**
TOTAL TIME: 30 MIN.

Grab the skewers, fire up the grill, and enjoy these easy and delicious kabobs, great for any night of the week.

½ cup bourbon

¼ cup fresh lemon juice

2 garlic cloves, minced

¼ cup olive oil, divided

2 tsp. chopped fresh rosemary, divided

I lb. boneless pork loin, cut into I ½-inch cubes

¾ cup bottled barbecue sauce

8 (10-inch) metal skewers

I tsp. table salt

½ tsp. freshly ground black pepper

2 large peaches, unpeeled and cut into 8 wedges each

I large green bell pepper, cut into I ½-inch pieces

1. Preheat grill to 350° to 400° (medium-high) heat. Whisk together first 3 ingredients, 2 Tbsp. olive oil, and I tsp. rosemary; reserve ¼ cup. Pour remaining mixture into a large shallow dish or zip-top plastic freezer bag; add pork, turning to coat. Cover or seal, and let stand 10 minutes.

2. Meanwhile, cook barbecue sauce and reserved ¼ cup mixture in a medium saucepan over medium heat, stirring occasionally, 3 minutes or until bubbly. Remove from heat.

3. Remove pork from marinade, discarding marinade. Thread pork onto skewers, leaving a ⅛-inch space between pieces. Sprinkle pork with salt and pepper.

4. Thread peaches and bell peppers alternately onto other skewers, leaving a ⅛-inch space between pieces. Drizzle with remaining 2 Tbsp. olive oil, and sprinkle with remaining I tsp. rosemary.

5. Grill pork, covered with grill lid, 7 to 8 minutes on each side or until done, turning occasionally and brushing pork with barbecue sauce mixture during last 5 minutes of grilling. At the same time, grill fruit-and-vegetable kabobs, covered with grill lid, 4 minutes on each side or until bell peppers are crisp-tender.

grocery guide:

❏ I (750-milliliter) bottle bourbon
❏ 2 lemons
❏ I small garlic bulb
❏ I bunch fresh rosemary
❏ I lb. boneless pork loin
❏ 8 (10-inch) metal skewers
❏ 2 large peaches
❏ I large green bell pepper

Easy Lasagna

**MAKES: 6 TO 8 SERVINGS HANDS-ON TIME: 15 MIN.
TOTAL TIME: 1 HOUR, 25 MIN.**

1 lb. mild Italian sausage	2 (26-oz.) jars pasta sauce*
1 (15-oz.) container part-skim ricotta cheese	9 no-boil lasagna noodles*
¼ cup refrigerated ready-made pesto*	4 cups (16 oz.) shredded Italian three-cheese blend or mozzarella cheese
1 large egg, lightly beaten	

1. Preheat oven to 350°.

2. Remove and discard casings from sausage. Cook sausage in a large skillet over medium heat, stirring often, 5 to 6 minutes or until meat crumbles and is no longer pink; drain.

3. Stir together ricotta cheese, pesto, and egg.

4. Spread half of 1 jar pasta sauce evenly in a lightly greased 13- x 9-inch baking dish. Layer with 3 lasagna noodles (noodles should not touch each other or sides of dish), half of ricotta mixture, half of sausage, 1 cup three-cheese blend, and remaining half of 1 jar pasta sauce. Repeat layers. Top with remaining 3 noodles and second jar of pasta sauce, covering noodles completely. Sprinkle evenly with remaining 2 cups three-cheese blend.

5. Bake, covered, at 350° for 40 minutes. Uncover and bake 15 more minutes or until edges are golden and cheese is bubbly. Let stand 15 minutes.

  * We tested with Buitoni Pesto with Basil, Classico Tomato & Basil spaghetti sauce, and Barilla Lasagne Oven-Ready noodles.

Vanessa's Savvy Secret: Scrape the layer of solidified oil from the top of the container of pesto, and discard. Then measure the pesto.

grocery guide:

❏ 1 lb. mild Italian sausage
❏ 1 (15-oz.) container part-skim ricotta cheese
❏ 1 (9-oz.) box no-boil lasagna noodles

"Jefferson" Virginia Ham Pasta

MAKES: 6 TO 8 SERVINGS   **HANDS-ON TIME: 30 min.**
TOTAL TIME: 30 min.

Our nod to the Virginia wine country and Thomas Jefferson's love of pasta.

2	(8.8-oz.) packages strozzapreti pasta	1	cup Viognier or dry white wine*
¼	lb. country ham, cut into ⅛-inch-thick strips (about ¾ cup)	½	cup frozen sweet peas
		⅓	cup coarsely chopped fresh flat-leaf parsley
2	Tbsp. olive oil	¼	cup heavy cream
3	shallots, thinly sliced	3	Tbsp. butter
8	oz. assorted wild mushrooms, sliced	¼	tsp. black pepper
1	garlic clove, thinly sliced	1	cup freshly grated pecorino Romano cheese, divided

1. Prepare pasta according to package directions.

2. Meanwhile, sauté ham strips in hot oil in a large skillet over medium heat 2 minutes or until lightly browned and crisp. Add shallots; sauté 1 minute. Add mushrooms and garlic, and cook, stirring often, 2 minutes or until mushrooms are tender. Stir in wine, and cook 5 minutes or until reduced by half.

3. Add peas, next 4 ingredients, and ½ cup cheese, stirring until cheese begins to melt and cream begins to thicken. Stir in hot cooked pasta, and toss until coated. Serve immediately with remaining ½ cup cheese.

*We tested with Jefferson Vineyards Viognier.

grocery guide:

- ❏ 2 (8.8-oz.) packages strozzapreti pasta
- ❏ ¼ lb. country ham
- ❏ 3 shallots
- ❏ 1 (8-oz.) package assorted wild mushrooms
- ❏ 1 small garlic bulb
- ❏ 1 bunch fresh flat-leaf parsley
- ❏ 1 (8-oz.) container heavy cream
- ❏ 1 (8-oz.) wedge pecorino Romano cheese

Country Ham Carbonara

MAKES: 4 servings **HANDS-ON TIME: 30 MIN.**
TOTAL TIME: 30 MIN.

Hearty, not heavy, is key in this savory Italian one-dish pasta. Serve immediately for the best flavor.

1 (9-oz.) package refrigerated fettuccine	2 pasteurized egg yolks
¾ cup chopped country ham	½ cup (2 oz.) freshly shredded Parmesan cheese
2 Tbsp. olive oil	3 Tbsp. chopped fresh chives
2 shallots, thinly sliced	3 Tbsp. chopped fresh parsley
2 garlic cloves, pressed	½ tsp. freshly cracked pepper

1. Cook pasta according to package directions; drain, reserving 1½ cups hot pasta water.

2. Cook ham in hot oil in a large skillet over medium-high heat 4 to 5 minutes or until crisp. Remove ham, reserving drippings in skillet. Drain on paper towels.

3. Sauté shallots in hot drippings 3 to 4 minutes or until tender. Stir in garlic; sauté 1 minute. Add reserved pasta water to shallots and garlic; bring to boil. Stir in hot cooked pasta, and remove from heat. Stir in egg yolks, 1 at a time.

4. Reduce heat to medium, and cook, stirring constantly, 2 to 3 minutes or until creamy. Remove from heat; add cooked ham, Parmesan cheese, and remaining ingredients. Sprinkle with additional Parmesan cheese, if desired. Serve immediately.

grocery guide:

- ❏ 1 (9-oz.) package refrigerated fettuccine
- ❏ ¼ lb. country ham
- ❏ 2 shallots
- ❏ 1 small garlic bulb
- ❏ ½ dozen pasteurized eggs
- ❏ 1 (5-oz.) package freshly shredded Parmesan cheese
- ❏ 1 (0.75-oz.) package fresh chives
- ❏ 1 bunch fresh parsley

Chicken Cobbler Casserole

MAKES: 4 SERVINGS **HANDS-ON TIME: 20 MIN.**
TOTAL TIME: 35 MIN.

6	Tbsp. butter, melted and divided	1	cup white wine
4	cups sourdough rolls, cubed	1	(10 ¾-oz.) can cream of mushroom soup
⅓	cup grated Parmesan cheese	2 ½	cups shredded cooked chicken
2	Tbsp. chopped fresh parsley		
2	medium-size sweet onions, sliced	½	cup jarred roasted red bell peppers, drained and chopped
1	(8-oz.) package sliced fresh mushrooms		

1. Preheat oven to 400°.

2. Stir together 4 Tbsp. melted butter and next 3 ingredients; set aside.

3. Sauté onions in remaining 2 Tbsp. butter in a large skillet over medium-high heat 15 minutes or until golden brown. Add mushrooms, and sauté 5 minutes.

4. Stir in wine and next 3 ingredients; cook, stirring constantly, 5 minutes or until bubbly. Spoon mixture into a lightly greased 9-inch square baking dish; top evenly with bread mixture.

5. Bake at 400° for 15 minutes or until golden brown and bubbly.

grocery guide:

- ❏ 4 sourdough rolls
- ❏ 1 bunch fresh parsley
- ❏ 2 medium-size sweet onions
- ❏ 1 (8-oz.) package sliced fresh mushrooms

Grilled Chicken Burritos

MAKES: 4 SERVINGS **HANDS-ON TIME: 30 MIN.**
TOTAL TIME: I HOUR, 10 MIN.

3   skinned and boned chicken breasts
½   tsp. table salt
¼   tsp. black pepper
2   (10-oz.) cans diced tomatoes with green chiles, divided
I   (19.75-oz.) can black beans, drained, rinsed, and divided
2   cups (8 oz.) shredded Monterey Jack cheese, divided

8   (8-inch) soft taco-size flour tortillas
I   (10-oz.) can green enchilada sauce
2   avocados, sliced
I   (8-oz.) container sour cream
Topping: sliced green onions

1. Preheat oven to 350°.

2. Sprinkle chicken breasts with salt and black pepper.

3. Coat cold cooking grate of grill with cooking spray and place on grill. Preheat grill to 350° to 400° (medium-high) heat. Place chicken on cooking grate, and grill 10 minutes on each side or until done.

4. Coarsely chop chicken, and place in a large bowl. Stir in I can tomatoes with green chiles, half of black beans, and I cup cheese.

5. Spoon chicken mixture just below center of each tortilla. Fold opposite sides of tortilla over filling, and roll up. Place, seam sides down, in a 13- x 9-inch baking dish. Top with enchilada sauce, remaining tomatoes with green chiles, black beans, and cheese.

6. Bake at 350° for 30 minutes. Remove from oven, and let stand 10 minutes. Top each serving with green onions, avocado slices, and sour cream.

grocery guide:

❑ 3 skinned and boned chicken breasts
❑ 2 avocados
❑ I bunch green onions

Roast Chicken

**MAKES: 4 TO 6 SERVINGS   HANDS-ON TIME: 20 MIN.
TOTAL TIME: 1 HOUR, 35 MIN.**

Roasted with lemon, dried rosemary, and seasoned pepper, this savory chicken will definitely impress your guests.

grocery guide:

- ❏ 1 (4- to 5-lb.) whole chicken
- ❏ 1 lemon

1 (4- to 5-lb.) whole chicken	1 tsp. dried rosemary*
1½ tsp. kosher salt, divided	1 Tbsp. olive oil
1 lemon half	1 Tbsp. butter, melted
1 tsp. seasoned pepper	

1. Preheat oven to 450°. If applicable, remove neck and giblets from chicken, and reserve for another use. Rinse chicken with cold water, and drain cavity well. Pat dry with paper towels. Sprinkle ½ tsp. salt inside cavity. Place lemon half inside cavity.

2. Stir together pepper, rosemary, and remaining 1 tsp. salt. Brush outside of chicken with oil. Rub 2½ tsp. pepper mixture into skin. Sprinkle remaining pepper mixture over both sides of breast. Place chicken, breast side up, on a lightly greased wire rack in a lightly greased shallow roasting pan. Add ¾ cup water to pan.

3. Bake at 450° for 20 minutes. Reduce heat to 375°; bake 30 minutes. Baste chicken with pan juices; drizzle with melted butter. Bake 15 to 25 minutes or until a meat thermometer inserted in thigh registers 165°, shielding with aluminum foil to prevent excessive browning, if necessary. Remove chicken from oven, and baste with pan juices. Let stand 10 minutes before slicing.

*We tested with McCormick Gourmet Collection Crushed Rosemary.

Quick Chicken Piccata

MAKES: 4 SERVINGS   **HANDS-ON TIME: 30 MIN.**
TOTAL TIME: 30 MIN.

1	lb. skinned and boned chicken breasts	¼	cup chicken broth
½	tsp. table salt	3	Tbsp. fresh lemon juice
½	tsp. black pepper	2	Tbsp. butter
½	cup Italian-seasoned breadcrumbs	2	Tbsp. chopped fresh parsley
2	Tbsp. olive oil	1	(12-oz.) package angel hair pasta, cooked

Garnish: lemon wedges

1. Cut each chicken breast in half horizontally. Place between 2 sheets of heavy-duty plastic wrap; flatten to ¼-inch thickness, using a rolling pin or the flat side of a meat mallet.

2. Sprinkle chicken evenly with salt and pepper; lightly dredge in breadcrumbs.

3. Cook half of chicken in 1 Tbsp. hot oil in a large nonstick skillet over medium-high heat 2 minutes on each side or until golden brown and done. Remove chicken to a serving platter, and cover with aluminum foil. Repeat procedure with remaining chicken and 1 Tbsp. olive oil.

4. Add broth and lemon juice to skillet, and cook, stirring to loosen browned bits from bottom of skillet, until sauce is slightly thickened. Remove from heat; add butter and parsley, stirring until butter melts. Pour sauce over chicken, and serve over warm noodles.

grocery guide:

- ❏ 1 lb. skinned and boned chicken breasts
- ❏ 3 lemons
- ❏ 1 bunch fresh parsley
- ❏ 1 (12 oz.) package angel hair pasta

Skillet Chicken Pot Pie

**MAKES: 6 TO 8 SERVINGS   HANDS-ON TIME: 30 MIN.
TOTAL TIME: 1 HOUR., 30 MIN.**

Refrigerated piecrusts speed up the preparation of this classic comfort dish.

Filling:
- ⅓ cup butter
- ⅓ cup all-purpose flour
- 1½ cups chicken broth
- 1½ cups milk
- 1½ tsp. Creole seasoning
- 2 Tbsp. butter
- 1 large sweet onion, diced
- 1 (8-oz.) package sliced fresh mushrooms

- 4 cups shredded cooked chicken
- 2 cups frozen cubed hash browns
- 1 cup matchstick carrots
- 1 cup frozen small sweet peas
- ⅓ cup chopped fresh parsley

Pastry Crust:
- 1 (14.1-oz.) package refrigerated piecrusts
- 1 egg white

1. Prepare Filling: Preheat oven to 350°. Melt ⅓ cup butter in a large saucepan over medium heat; add flour, and cook, whisking constantly, 1 minute. Gradually add chicken broth and milk, and cook, whisking constantly, 6 to 7 minutes or until thickened and bubbly. Remove from heat, and stir in Creole seasoning.

2. Melt 2 Tbsp. butter in a large Dutch oven over medium-high heat; add onion and mushrooms, and sauté 10 minutes or until tender. Stir in chicken, next 4 ingredients, and sauce.

3. Prepare Pastry Crust: Place 1 piecrust in a lightly greased 10-inch skillet. Spoon chicken mixture over piecrust, and top with remaining piecrust.

4. Whisk egg white until foamy; brush top of piecrust with egg white. Cut 4 to 5 slits in top of pie for steam to escape.

5. Bake at 350° for 1 hour to 1 hour and 5 minutes or until golden brown and bubbly.

grocery guide:

- ☐ Creole seasoning
- ☐ 1 large sweet onion
- ☐ 1 (8-oz.) package sliced fresh mushrooms
- ☐ 1 (32-oz.) package frozen cubed hash browns
- ☐ 1 bunch fresh parsley
- ☐ 1 (16-oz) package matchstick carrots

Poblano Chicken Tacos

MAKES: 6 SERVINGS **HANDS-ON TIME: 22 MIN.**
TOTAL TIME: 40 MIN.

1	large poblano pepper
½	English cucumber, coarsely chopped
1	cup grape tomatoes, quartered
2	Tbsp. chopped red onion
1	garlic clove, minced
½	tsp. table salt
3	Tbsp. fresh lime juice, divided

4	Tbsp. olive oil, divided
1	Tbsp. mango-lime seafood seasoning*
1 ½	lb. skinned and boned chicken breasts
12	(6-inch) fajita-size corn tortillas, warmed
	Lime wedges
	Fresh cilantro leaves (optional)

1. Preheat grill to 350° to 400° (medium-high) heat. Grill pepper, covered with grill lid, 3 to 4 minutes or until pepper looks blistered, turning once. Place pepper in a large zip-top plastic freezer bag; seal and let stand 10 minutes to loosen skin. Peel pepper; remove and discard seeds. Coarsely chop.

2. Combine pepper, cucumber, next 4 ingredients, 2 Tbsp. lime juice, and 2 Tbsp. olive oil in a large bowl.

3. Whisk together seasoning, remaining 1 Tbsp. lime juice, and remaining 2 Tbsp. olive oil in a large shallow dish or zip-top plastic freezer bag; add chicken, turning to coat. Cover or seal, and chill 5 minutes, turning once. Remove chicken from marinade, discarding marinade.

4. Grill chicken, covered with grill lid, 3 to 4 minutes on each side or until done. Cool 5 minutes. Coarsely chop or shred chicken.

5. Serve chicken and salsa in warm tortillas with lime wedges.

 * We tested with Weber Mango Lime Seafood Seasoning.

Gourmet Flip: Top with crumbled queso fresco (fresh Mexican cheese) for a south-of-the-border flair.

grocery guide:

- ❑ 1 large poblano pepper
- ❑ 1 English cucumber
- ❑ 1 pt. grape tomatoes
- ❑ 1 small red onion
- ❑ 1 small garlic bulb
- ❑ 3 limes
- ❑ 1 (2.75-oz.) jar mango-lime seafood seasoning
- ❑ 1 ½ lb. skinned and boned chicken breasts
- ❑ Optional: 1 bunch fresh cilantro

Grilled Chicken-Vegetable Kabobs

MAKES: 6 SERVINGS   **HANDS-ON TIME: 30 MIN.**
TOTAL TIME: 1 HOUR, INCLUDING CHILL TIME

½ cup red pepper jelly

¼ tsp. dried crushed red pepper

⅔ cup red wine vinegar, divided

1 tsp. table salt, divided

1 tsp. freshly ground black pepper, divided

1½ lb. skinned and boned chicken breasts, cut into 1-inch pieces

1 medium-size red onion, cut into 8 wedges

2 medium-size yellow squash, cut into 1-inch pieces

24 small fresh okra (about ¾ lb.)

8 (12-inch) metal skewers, divided

¼ cup olive oil

1. Whisk together pepper jelly, red pepper, ⅓ cup red wine vinegar, and ½ tsp. each salt and black pepper in a shallow dish or zip-top plastic freezer bag. Add chicken, turning to coat. Cover or seal, and chill 30 minutes, turning occasionally.

2. Place vegetables in a shallow pan. Whisk together olive oil and remaining ⅓ cup vinegar, ½ tsp. salt, and ½ tsp. black pepper. Pour over vegetables, and chill 30 minutes.

3. Preheat grill to 350° to 400° (medium-high) heat. Remove chicken from marinade, discarding marinade. Thread vegetables and chicken alternately onto 8 skewers, leaving a ⅛-inch space between pieces.

4. Grill kabobs, covered with grill lid, 6 to 8 minutes on each side or until chicken is done and vegetables are crisp-tender.

grocery guide:

- ❏ 1 (10-oz.) jar red pepper jelly
- ❏ 1½ lb. skinned and boned chicken breasts
- ❏ 1 medium-size red onion
- ❏ 2 medium-size yellow squash
- ❏ 24 small fresh okra (about ¾ lb.)
- ❏ 8 (12-inch) metal skewers

White Lightning Chicken Chili

MAKES: 11 ½ CUPS **HANDS-ON TIME: 30 MIN.**
TOTAL TIME: 30 MIN.

White Lightning Chicken Chili gets its name because it takes only 30 minutes from start to finish to get this one-dish meal to the table. Don't drain the chopped green chiles or navy beans. Serve chili with cornbread.

1	large sweet onion, diced	1	(1.25-oz.) package white chicken chili seasoning mix*
2	garlic cloves, minced		
2	Tbsp. olive oil	3	(16-oz.) cans navy beans
4	cups shredded cooked chicken		Toppings: Avocado-Mango Salsa,
2	(14-oz.) cans chicken broth		sour cream, shredded
2	(4.5-oz.) cans chopped green chiles		Monterey Jack cheese, fresh cilantro leaves

Sauté onion and garlic in hot oil in a large Dutch oven over medium-high heat 5 minutes or until onion is tender. Stir in chicken, next 3 ingredients, and 2 cans navy beans. Coarsely mash remaining can navy beans, and stir into chicken mixture. Bring to a boil, stirring often; cover, reduce heat to medium-low, and simmer, stirring occasionally, 10 minutes. Serve with desired toppings.

* We tested with McCormick White Chicken Chili Seasoning Mix.

grocery guide:

- ❏ 1 large sweet onion
- ❏ 1 small garlic bulb
- ❏ 1 (1.25-oz.) package white chicken chili seasoning mix
- ❏ 3 (16-oz.) cans navy beans
- ❏ Optional: 1 bunch fresh cilantro

Avocado-Mango Salsa

MAKES: ABOUT 2 CUPS   **HANDS-ON TIME: 10 MIN.**
TOTAL TIME: 10 MIN.

Serve this salsa as a topping on your favorite white chili, or pair it with chips for a stand-alone appetizer.

1	large avocado, cubed	2	Tbsp. chopped fresh cilantro
1	cup diced fresh mango	2	Tbsp. fresh lime juice
⅓	cup diced red onion		

Stir together all ingredients.

grocery guide:

❏ 1 large avocado
❏ 1 mango
❏ 1 small red onion
❏ 1 bunch fresh cilantro
❏ 2 limes

King Ranch Chicken Mac and Cheese

MAKES: 6 SERVINGS   **HANDS-ON TIME: 45 MIN.**
TOTAL TIME: 45 MIN.

grocery guide:

- ❏ I (I6-oz.) package cellentani pasta
- ❏ I medium onion
- ❏ I green bell pepper
- ❏ I (8-oz.) package pasteurized prepared cheese product

½ (16-oz.) package cellentani pasta
2 Tbsp. butter
1 medium onion, diced
1 green bell pepper, diced
1 (10-oz.) can diced tomatoes and green chiles
1 (8-oz.) package pasteurized prepared cheese product, cubed
3 cups chopped cooked chicken
1 (10 ¾-oz.) can cream of chicken soup
½ cup sour cream
1 tsp. chili powder
½ tsp. ground cumin
1 ½ cups (6 oz.) shredded Cheddar cheese

1. Preheat oven to 350°. Prepare pasta according to package directions.

2. Meanwhile, melt butter in a large Dutch oven over medium-high heat. Add onion and bell pepper, and sauté 5 minutes or until tender. Stir in tomatoes and green chiles and prepared cheese product; cook, stirring constantly, 2 minutes or until cheese melts. Stir in chicken, next 4 ingredients, and hot cooked pasta until blended. Spoon mixture into a lightly greased 10-inch cast-iron skillet or 11- x 7-inch baking dish; sprinkle with shredded Cheddar cheese.

3. Bake at 350° for 25 to 30 minutes or until bubbly.

Grilled Chicken and Garden Salsa

MAKES: 4 SERVINGS   **HANDS-ON TIME: 30 MIN.**
TOTAL TIME: 30 MIN.

4	skinned and boned chicken breasts	1	tsp. fresh lemon juice
½	tsp. table salt	2	medium zucchini, cut lengthwise into ½-inch-wide strips
½	tsp. freshly ground black pepper	1	small sweet onion, sliced
3	Tbsp. freshly grated Parmesan cheese	1	medium-size red bell pepper, quartered
3	Tbsp. mayonnaise	2	Tbsp. olive oil
2	tsp. lemon zest	½	cup small fresh basil leaves

1. Preheat grill to 300° to 350° (medium) heat. Sprinkle chicken with salt and black pepper. Combine cheese and next 3 ingredients. Brush chicken with cheese mixture.

2. Toss zucchini, onion, and bell pepper in olive oil.

3. Grill chicken, covered with grill lid, 7 to 10 minutes on each side or until done. At the same time, grill vegetable mixture, covered with grill lid, 2 to 3 minutes or until crisp-tender. Chop vegetable mixture, and toss with basil. Add salt and pepper to taste. Serve vegetable mixture with grilled chicken.

grocery guide:

- ❏ 4 skinned and boned chicken breasts
- ❏ 1 lemon
- ❏ 2 medium zucchini
- ❏ 1 small sweet onion
- ❏ 1 medium-size red bell pepper
- ❏ 1 bunch fresh basil

Chicken Fried Rice

Makes: about 2 cups   **Hands-On Time: 10 min.**

Total Time: 10 min.

3	Tbsp. vegetable oil, divided	2	cups chopped cooked chicken
4	large eggs, lightly beaten	4	cups cooked basmati rice
¾	cup diced onion	⅓	cup soy sauce
¾	cup diced red bell pepper		2 to 3 tsp. Asian hot chili sauce
1	lb. haricots verts (thin green		(such as Sriracha)
	beans), trimmed and cut into		Toppings: sliced green onions,
	1½-inch pieces (about 2 cups)		toasted sliced almonds

grocery guide:

- ☐ 1 onion
- ☐ 1 red bell pepper
- ☐ 1 lb. haricots verts
- ☐ 1 deli-roasted chicken
- ☐ basmati rice
- ☐ 1 bunch green onions
- ☐ toasted sliced almonds

1. Heat 1 Tbsp. oil in a large skillet over medium-high heat 1 minute; add eggs, and cook, gently stirring, 1 to 2 minutes or until softly scrambled. Remove eggs from skillet; chop.

2. Heat remaining 2 Tbsp. oil in skillet; add onion, bell pepper, and green beans, and stir-fry 3 to 4 minutes or until vegetables are crisp-tender. Add chicken, and stir-fry 2 minutes. Add rice, soy sauce, and hot chili sauce; stir-fry 3 to 4 minutes or until thoroughly heated. Stir in scrambled eggs; sprinkle with desired toppings.

Gourmet Flip: Substitute cooked shrimp for the cooked chicken, if desired.

Shrimp Succotash

MAKES: 4 TO 6 SERVINGS   **HANDS-ON TIME: 45 MIN.**
TOTAL TIME: 45 MIN.

2	cups fresh butter beans (about ½ lb.)*	1	jalapeño pepper, seeded and minced
1¼	tsp. kosher salt, divided	½	cup diced red bell pepper
1½	lb. peeled and deveined, extra-large raw shrimp	2	garlic cloves, minced
2	Tbsp. olive oil, divided	1	medium-size heirloom tomato, seeded and diced
¼	tsp. freshly ground black pepper	1	cup fresh corn kernels (2 ears)
1	cup sliced fresh okra	¼	cup small fresh basil leaves
1	small sweet onion, chopped	1	Tbsp. butter

1. Rinse, sort, and drain butter beans.

2. Bring butter beans, 1 tsp. salt, and 4 cups water to a boil in a saucepan over medium-high heat. Reduce heat to medium-low, and simmer, stirring occasionally, 35 minutes or until beans are tender; drain.

3. Meanwhile, combine shrimp, 1 Tbsp. oil, ¼ tsp. black pepper, and remaining ¼ tsp. salt in a bowl, tossing to coat. Heat a grill pan over medium-high heat; cook shrimp 4 to 5 minutes or just until shrimp turn pink. Transfer to a plate, and cover loosely with aluminum foil to keep warm.

4. Heat remaining 1 Tbsp. oil in a large skillet over medium heat. Add okra; cook 3 minutes or until lightly browned. Stir in onion and next 3 ingredients; cook 3 minutes or until vegetables are tender. Add tomato and corn; sauté 3 to 4 minutes or until corn is tender. Stir in basil, butter, shrimp, and butter beans. Cook 1 minute or until butter is melted and mixture is thoroughly heated. Season with salt and pepper to taste. Serve immediately.

    * Frozen butter beans may be substituted. Omit Step 1.

Vanessa's Savvy Secret: This is a fantastic light summer meal. It's especially delicious with Silver Queen corn and heirloom tomatoes, but you can use your favorite varieties.

grocery guide:

- ❏ ½ lb. fresh butter beans
- ❏ 1½ lb. peeled and deveined, extra-large raw shrimp
- ❏ 8 large okra
- ❏ 1 small sweet onion
- ❏ 1 jalapeño pepper
- ❏ 1 large red bell pepper
- ❏ 1 small garlic bulb
- ❏ 1 medium-size heirloom tomato
- ❏ 2 ears fresh corn
- ❏ 1 bunch fresh basil

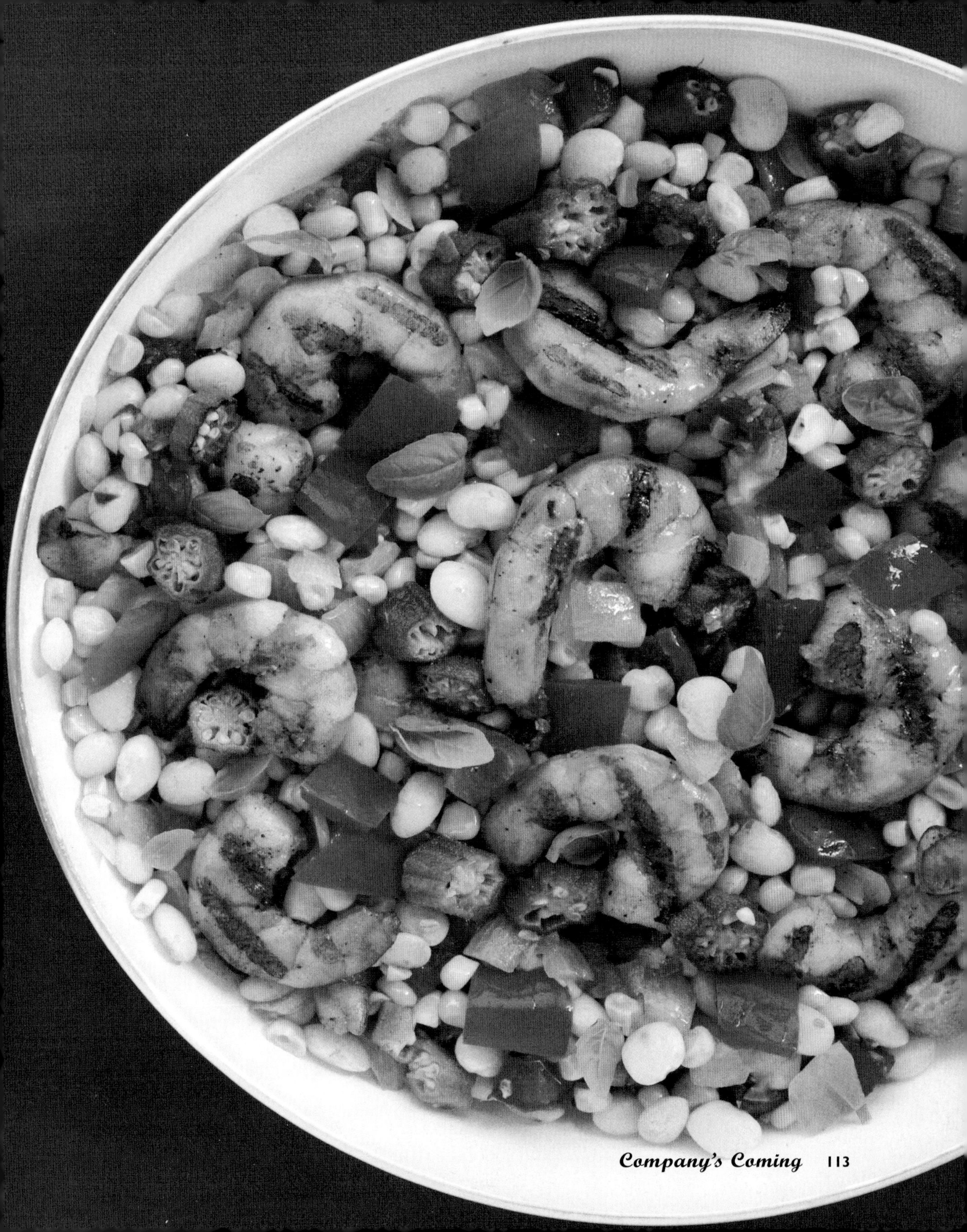

Spicy Fish Tacos with Mango Salsa and Guacamole

**MAKES: ABOUT 2 SERVINGS HANDS-ON TIME: 20 MIN.
TOTAL TIME: 20 MIN.**

6 (6-oz.) flounder fillets
1 lime
2 Tbsp. chili powder
2 tsp. table salt
2 tsp. ground cumin
½ tsp. ground red pepper
1 ½ cups plain yellow cornmeal
Vegetable oil

4 to 6 (8-inch) soft taco-size flour
   or corn tortillas, warmed
Mango salsa
Guacamole
Toppings: shredded iceberg
   lettuce, chopped tomato
Garnishes: lime wedges, fresh
   cilantro leaves

grocery guide:

❑ 6 (6-oz.) flounder fillets
❑ 1 lime
❑ plain yellow cornmeal
❑ 1 (16-oz.) jar mango salsa
❑ 1 (7-oz.) package refrigerated
   guacamole
❑ Optional: shredded iceberg
   lettuce, chopped tomatoes,
   lime wedges, fresh cilantro

1. Place fish in a shallow dish. Squeeze juice of 1 lime over fillets.

2. Combine chili powder and next 3 ingredients. Sprinkle 1 ½ Tbsp. seasoning mixture evenly over fish, coating both sides of fillets. Reserve remaining seasoning mixture.

3. Combine cornmeal and reserved seasoning mixture in a shallow dish. Dredge fish fillets in cornmeal mixture, shaking off excess.

4. Pour oil to depth of 1 ½ inches in a Dutch oven; heat to 350°. Fry fillets, in batches, 2 to 3 minutes or until golden brown. Drain fillets on wire racks over paper towels.

5. Break each fillet into chunks, using a fork. Place fish in warmed tortillas, and serve with mango salsa, guacamole, and desired toppings.

Stretch Your Budget: Tilapia or shrimp also work well in this recipe. Purchase whichever is on sale.

Grilled Blackened Shrimp Kabobs

MAKES: 4 TO 6 SERVINGS   **HANDS-ON TIME: 30 MIN.**
TOTAL TIME: 30 MIN.

36	unpeeled, large raw shrimp (about I lb.)	36	fresh blackberries
I	tsp. olive oil	18	fresh mango slices
2	tsp. Cajun blackened seasoning		Mint-Lime Drizzle (optional)
18	(6-inch) wooden skewers		Garnishes: lime wedges, fresh mint sprigs

1. Preheat grill to 350° to 400° (medium-high) heat. Peel shrimp, leaving tails on; devein, if desired.

2. Place shrimp in a large bowl, and drizzle with olive oil. Sprinkle with seasoning, and toss to coat.

3. Grill shrimp, covered with grill lid, 2 to 3 minutes on each side or just until shrimp turn pink.

4. Thread each skewer with 2 grilled shrimp, 2 blackberries, and I mango slice. Brush with Mint-Lime Drizzle.

Mint-Lime Drizzle

MAKES: ABOUT 2 CUPS   **HANDS-ON TIME: 10 MIN.**
TOTAL TIME: 10 MIN.

Mint-Lime Drizzle brightens the flavor of grilled seafood.

I	Tbsp. chopped fresh mint	I	Tbsp. olive oil
I	Tbsp. fresh lime juice	I	tsp. sugar

Stir together all ingredients.

grocery guide:

❏ 36 unpeeled, large raw shrimp (about I lb.)
❏ Cajun blackened seasoning
❏ 18 (6-inch) wooden skewers
❏ 2 pt. blackberries
❏ 2 large mangoes
❏ Optional: I lime
❏ I bunch fresh mint

grocery guide:

❏ I bunch fresh mint
❏ I lime

Beer-Battered Fried Fish

MAKES: 8 SERVINGS　　　**HANDS-ON TIME: 30 MIN.**
TOTAL TIME: 30 MIN.

grocery guide:

❑ 2 lb. grouper fillets
❑ 1 (12-oz.) bottle beer

Vegetable oil	1½ cups all-purpose flour
2　lb. grouper fillets, cut into pieces	1½ tsp. sugar
2　tsp. table salt, divided	1　(12-oz.) bottle beer
½　tsp. freshly ground black pepper	1　tsp. hot sauce
	Malt Vinegar Mignonette
	Buttermilk-Ranch-Herb Sauce

1. Pour oil to depth of 3 inches into a large Dutch oven; heat to 360°.

2. Meanwhile, sprinkle fish with 1 tsp. salt and black pepper.

3. Whisk together flour, sugar, and remaining 1 tsp. salt in a large bowl. Whisk in beer and hot sauce. Dip fish in batter, allowing excess batter to drip off.

4. Gently lower fish into hot oil using tongs (to prevent fish from sticking to Dutch oven). Fry fish, in 4 batches, 2 to 3 minutes on each side or until golden brown. Place fried fish on a wire rack in a jelly-roll pan; keep warm in a 200° oven until ready to serve. Serve with Malt Vinegar Mignonette and Buttermilk-Ranch-Herb Sauce.

Malt Vinegar Mignonette

MAKES: ABOUT 2 CUPS　　　**HANDS-ON TIME: 10 MIN.**
TOTAL TIME: 10 MIN.

grocery guide:

❑ 1 (12-oz.) bottle malt vinegar
❑ 1 large shallot

2　cups malt vinegar	½　tsp. freshly ground black pepper
1　large shallot, diced	

Stir together all ingredients in a small bowl. Serve immediately, or cover and chill up to 24 hours.

Buttermilk-Ranch-Herb Sauce

MAKES: ABOUT 2 CUPS   **HANDS-ON TIME: 10 MIN.**
TOTAL TIME: 10 MIN.

1	cup mayonnaise	3	Tbsp. fresh lemon juice
⅓	cup buttermilk	½	tsp. freshly ground black
1½	Tbsp. chopped fresh chives		pepper
2	tsp. Ranch dressing mix	¼	tsp. table salt
1	tsp. lemon zest		

Whisk together all ingredients. Serve immediately, or cover and chill up to 2 days.

grocery guide:

❑ 1 qt. buttermilk
❑ 1 (0.75-oz.) package fresh chives
❑ Ranch dressing mix
❑ 2 lemons

What's for Supper

Garden Tomato Sauce over Pasta

MAKES: ABOUT 3 CUPS **HANDS-ON TIME: 15 MIN.**
TOTAL TIME: 15 MIN.

We love this sauce as a meatless meal over hearty pasta. Or try it in lasagna or a meatball sub.

1 onion, diced (about 1 cup)	Freshly ground black pepper
1 Tbsp. olive oil	¼ cup dry red wine
1 garlic clove, minced	3 Tbsp. chopped fresh oregano or marjoram
4 medium-size heirloom tomatoes (about 2 lb.), cored and chopped	Hot cooked pasta
Kosher salt	Garnish: fresh oregano leaves

1. Sauté onion in hot oil in a Dutch oven over medium-high heat 3 minutes or until tender. Add garlic; sauté 1 minute. Add tomatoes, kosher salt, and freshly ground pepper to taste.

2. Cook, stirring often, 2 to 3 minutes or until tomatoes start to release their juices. Add wine, and cook, stirring occasionally, 5 to 8 minutes or until almost all liquid has evaporated.

3. Remove from heat, and stir in oregano. Serve sauce over hot cooked pasta. Refrigerate sauce in an airtight container up to 1 week, or freeze up to 1 month.

grocery guide:

❑ 1 onion
❑ 1 small garlic bulb
❑ 4 medium-size heirloom tomatoes
❑ 1 bunch fresh oregano or marjoram
❑ 1 (16 oz.) package pasta of choice

Black Bean Enchiladas

MAKES: 8 SERVINGS **HANDS-ON TIME: 15 MIN.**
TOTAL TIME: 45 MIN.

2   (15-oz.) cans black beans, drained and rinsed
1   tsp. chili powder
½   tsp. ground cumin
½   tsp. onion powder
½   tsp. garlic powder
1   (16-oz.) jar medium salsa
½   cup Monterey Jack queso dip
½   cup sour cream
8   (8-inch) soft taco-size flour tortillas

Toppings: shredded lettuce, chopped fresh cilantro, chopped tomato

1. Preheat oven to 350°. Mash 1 can of beans with a potato masher in a bowl; add remaining beans, chili powder, and next 3 ingredients, stirring until blended. Stir together salsa, queso dip, and sour cream in a bowl.

2. Spoon about ½ cup black bean mixture down center of each tortilla. Top each with 2 Tbsp. salsa mixture. Roll up tortillas, and place, seam sides down, in a lightly greased 13- x 9-inch baking dish. Pour remaining salsa mixture evenly over tortillas. Bake, covered, at 350° for 30 to 35 minutes or until thoroughly heated.

grocery guide:

❏ 1 (15-oz.) jar Monterey Jack queso dip
❏ 1 (8-oz.) package shredded lettuce
❏ 1 bunch cilantro and 1 tomato

make-ahead magic

Having dinner in the fridge or freezer can make the day less stressful.

Slow-Cooker Beef Brisket

MAKES: 6 SERVINGS **HANDS-ON TIME: 15 MIN.**
TOTAL TIME: 6 HOURS, 15 MIN.

2 medium onions, thinly sliced
2 celery ribs, thinly sliced
2 garlic cloves, pressed
1 (2- to 3-lb.) beef brisket*
2 tsp. table salt
1½ tsp. ground chipotle chile powder
1 cup coarsely chopped fresh cilantro
12 (6-inch) fajita-size flour tortillas
Toppings: shredded Pepper Jack cheese, sour cream, salsa, additional chopped fresh cilantro
Lime wedges

1. Place first 3 ingredients in a 6-qt. slow cooker.

2. Trim fat from brisket; cut brisket into 3-inch pieces. Rub brisket pieces evenly with salt and chipotle chile powder, and place on top of vegetables in slow cooker. Top with 1 cup cilantro.

3. Cover and cook on HIGH 6 to 8 hours or until brisket pieces shred easily with a fork.

4. Remove brisket from slow cooker, and cool slightly. Using 2 forks, shred meat into bite-size pieces. Return mixture to slow cooker. Serve in flour tortillas with desired toppings and lime wedges.

  * Note: Select a brisket that is uniform in thickness to make shredding the meat easier.

Kid Flip: Serve shredded brisket on top of tortillas with your choice of toppings for a creative taco night—use toppings like cheese and shredded lettuce for the kids and toppings like guacamole and fresh salsa for the adults.

grocery guide:

❏ 2 medium onions
❏ 1 bunch celery ribs
❏ 1 small garlic bulb
❏ 1 (2- to 3-lb.) beef brisket
❏ 1 (2-oz.) jar ground chipotle chile powder
❏ 1 bunch fresh cilantro
❏ Optional: limes

Simple Meatloaf

MAKES: 6 SERVINGS   **HANDS-ON TIME: 10 MIN.**
TOTAL TIME: 1 HOUR, 20 MIN.

1½	lb. lean ground beef	1½	tsp. table salt
¾	cup quick-cooking oats	¼	tsp. black pepper
¾	cup milk	⅓	cup ketchup
¼	cup chopped onion	2	Tbsp. brown sugar
1	large egg, lightly beaten	1	Tbsp. yellow mustard

1. Preheat oven to 350°.

2. Combine first 7 ingredients in a large bowl just until blended. Shape mixture into a lightly greased 9- x 5-inch loaf; place in an aluminum foil-lined broiler pan.

3. Stir together ketchup, brown sugar, and yellow mustard; pour evenly over meatloaf.

4. Bake at 350° for 1 to 1½ hours or until no longer pink in center. Let meatloaf stand 10 minutes before serving.

* Note: Wrap meatloaf in plastic wrap and aluminum foil, and freeze up to 1 month. Thaw in refrigerator overnight.

Stretch Your Budget: You can substitute ground chuck for the lean beef for a less expensive option.

grocery guide:

❏ 1½ lb. lean ground beef
❏ 1 onion

Slow-Cooker Beef Tacos

MAKES: 8 SERVINGS   **HANDS-ON TIME: 20 MIN.**
TOTAL TIME: 4 HOURS, 28 MIN.

2	lb. boneless beef chuck roast, cut into I-inch cubes	½	medium-size green bell pepper, cut into thin strips
I	tsp. table salt	I	tsp. ground cumin
I	Tbsp. vegetable oil	½	tsp. black pepper
I	Tbsp. chili powder	16	(8-inch) soft taco-size flour or corn tortillas, warmed
I	(6-oz.) can tomato paste		Toppings: sour cream, chopped red onion, chopped fresh cilantro
2	cups beef broth		
I	small white onion, sliced		
I	(8-oz.) can tomato sauce		

1. Sprinkle beef evenly with salt.

2. Cook beef, in batches, in hot oil in a Dutch oven over medium-high heat 5 to 7 minutes or until browned on all sides. Remove beef, reserving drippings in Dutch oven. Add chili powder to Dutch oven; cook, stirring constantly, I minute. Stir in tomato paste, and cook, stirring constantly, 2 minutes. Add broth, stirring to loosen browned bits from bottom of Dutch oven. Return beef to Dutch oven, and stir.

3. Place beef mixture in a 4½-quart slow cooker. Add onion and next 4 ingredients. Cook on HIGH 4 hours or on LOW 6 hours or until beef is tender. Serve with warm tortillas and desired toppings.

Make It Gourmet: Consider serving the tender beef over baked potatoes instead of in soft tortilla shells.

grocery guide:

- ❏ 2 lb. boneless beef chuck roast
- ❏ I (6-oz.) can tomato paste
- ❏ I small white onion
- ❏ I (8-oz.) can tomato sauce
- ❏ I medium-size green bell pepper
- ❏ Optional: I small red onion, I bunch fresh cilantro

Noodle-and-Spinach Casserole

MAKES: 8 TO 10 SERVINGS   HANDS-ON TIME: 25 MIN.
TOTAL TIME: 55 MIN.

1 (8-oz.) package wide egg noodles	2 cups (8 oz.) shredded Monterey Jack cheese
1 ½ lb. ground beef	1 ½ cups sour cream
2 garlic cloves, minced	1 large egg, lightly beaten
½ tsp. table salt	1 tsp. garlic salt
½ tsp. black pepper	1 ½ cups (6 oz.) shredded Parmesan cheese
1 (26-oz.) jar spaghetti sauce	Garnish: chopped fresh flat-leaf parsley
1 tsp. dried Italian seasoning	
1 (10-oz.) package frozen chopped spinach, thawed and drained	

1. Preheat oven to 350°.

2. Cook noodles according to package directions.

3. Brown ground beef and next 3 ingredients in a large nonstick skillet over medium heat, stirring, 6 to 8 minutes or until beef crumbles and is no longer pink. Drain and return to skillet. Stir in spaghetti sauce and Italian seasoning.

4. Combine spinach and next 4 ingredients. Fold in noodles; spoon mixture into a lightly greased 13- x 9-inch baking dish. Sprinkle with half of Parmesan cheese. Top with beef mixture and remaining Parmesan cheese.

5. Bake at 350° for 30 minutes or until bubbly and golden.

  * Note: To make ahead, bake as directed, cover, and freeze. Thaw overnight in refrigerator. Bake, covered, at 350° for 30 minutes. Uncover and bake 10 more minutes.

grocery guide:

❏ 1 ½ lb. ground beef
❏ 1 small garlic bulb
❏ 1 (26-oz.) jar spaghetti sauce
❏ 1 (10-oz.) package frozen chopped spinach
❏ Optional: 1 bunch fresh flat-leaf parsley

Our Best Barbecue

MAKES: 10 SERVINGS   **HANDS-ON TIME:** 20 MIN.
TOTAL TIME: 3 HOURS, 30 MIN.

1	(4-lb.) eye of round roast	¼	cup butter
1	tsp. table salt	¼	cup fresh lemon juice
3	(8-oz.) cans tomato sauce	2	Tbsp. Worcestershire sauce
1	(12-oz.) bottle chili sauce	½	tsp. dry mustard
1	medium onion, chopped	½	tsp. chili powder
½	cup white vinegar	½	tsp. paprika
¼	cup firmly packed brown sugar	10	hamburger buns
		Topping: dill pickle chips	

1. Place roast in large Dutch oven, and sprinkle with salt; add water to cover, and bring to a boil. Cover, reduce heat to medium, and simmer 2 hours or until tender, adding more water as needed after 1 hour.

2. Stir together tomato sauce and next 10 ingredients in a large saucepan; bring to a boil. Reduce heat to low, and simmer 1 hour, stirring occasionally.

3. Remove roast from Dutch oven, and let stand 10 minutes before serving. Shred or slice meat, and serve with hamburger buns and sauce. Add dill pickle chips, if desired.

 * Note: To make ahead, freeze both the meat and the sauce. To reheat, place in a 13- x 9-inch baking dish. Cover and bake at 350° for 30 minutes or until bubbly.

grocery guide:

❏ 1 (4-lb.) eye of round roast
❏ 3 (8-oz.) cans tomato sauce
❏ 1 (12-oz.) bottle chili sauce
❏ 1 medium onion
❏ 2 lemons
❏ 10 hamburger buns
❏ 1 (12-oz.) jar dill pickle chips

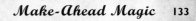

Slow-Cooker Mustard Barbecued Pork

MAKES: 10 TO 12 SERVINGS   **HANDS-ON TIME: 20 MIN.**
TOTAL TIME: 8 HOURS, 35 MIN.

⅓ cup firmly packed light brown sugar

2 ½ tsp. table salt

1 ½ tsp. garlic powder

1 ½ tsp. paprika

1 tsp. onion powder

½ tsp. ground red pepper

1 (4- to 5-lb.) bone-in pork shoulder roast (Boston butt)

1 cup yellow mustard

⅓ cup honey

¼ cup apple cider vinegar

1 ½ tsp. Worcestershire sauce

1 (15-oz.) package slider miniature sandwich buns

Lowcountry Slaw

1. Stir together first 6 ingredients. Rub brown sugar mixture over roast; place roast in a lightly greased 6-qt. slow cooker.

2. Whisk together mustard and next 3 ingredients. Pour mustard mixture over top of roast. Cover and cook on LOW 8 to 10 hours (or on HIGH 4 to 6 hours) or until meat shreds easily with a fork. Let stand 15 minutes. Shred pork with a fork; stir until sauce is incorporated.

3. Bake slider buns according to package directions. Spoon pork and Lowcountry Slaw evenly onto buns.

Lowcountry Slaw

MAKES: 10 TO 12 SERVINGS   **HANDS-ON TIME: 10 MIN.**
TOTAL TIME: 10 MIN.

¼ cup apple cider vinegar

¼ cup canola oil

2 Tbsp. mayonnaise

1 Tbsp. honey

½ tsp. table salt

¼ tsp. black pepper

¼ tsp. celery seeds

1 (16-oz.) package shredded coleslaw mix

1 cup sliced pickled okra

2 Tbsp. pickled okra juice

Whisk together first 7 ingredients in a large bowl. Stir in coleslaw mix, pickled okra, and pickled okra juice. Serve immediately, or chill up to 24 hours.

grocery guide:

❑ 1 (4- to 5-lb.) bone-in pork shoulder roast (Boston butt)

❑ Celery seeds

❑ 1 (16-oz.) bag shredded coleslaw mix

❑ 1 (16-oz.) jar pickled okra

❑ 1 (15 oz.) package slider miniature sandwich buns

Pizza Spaghetti Casserole

MAKES: 6 servings　　**HANDS-ON TIME: 30 MIN.**
TOTAL TIME: 1 HOUR, 10 MIN.

12　oz. uncooked spaghetti
½　tsp. table salt
1　(1-lb.) package mild ground
　　pork sausage
2　oz. turkey pepperoni slices
　　(about 30), cut in half

1　(26-oz.) jar tomato-and-basil
　　pasta sauce
¼　cup grated Parmesan cheese
1　(8-oz.) package shredded
　　Italian three-cheese blend

1. Preheat oven to 350°.

2. Cook spaghetti with salt according to package directions. Drain well, and place in a lightly greased 13- x 9-inch baking dish.

3. Brown sausage in a large skillet over medium-high heat, stirring occasionally, 5 minutes or until meat crumbles and is no longer pink. Drain and set aside. Wipe skillet clean. Add pepperoni, and cook over medium-high heat, stirring occasionally, 4 minutes or until slightly crisp.

4. Top spaghetti in baking dish with sausage; pour pasta sauce over sausage. Arrange half of pepperoni slices evenly over pasta sauce. Sprinkle evenly with cheeses. Arrange remaining half of pepperoni slices evenly over cheese. Cover with nonstick or lightly greased aluminum foil.

5. Bake at 350° for 30 minutes; remove foil, and bake 10 more minutes or until cheese is melted and just begins to brown.

　** Note: To make ahead, freeze the unbaked casserole up to one month. Thaw overnight in the refrigerator, and let stand at room temperature 30 minutes. Bake as directed.

Vanessa's Savvy Secret: Use turkey pepperoni in this recipe rather than regular to make it less greasy.

grocery guide:

❏ 1 (1-lb.) package mild ground
　　pork sausage
❏ 1 (6-oz.) package turkey
　　pepperoni slices

Kale-and-Sausage Hand Pies

MAKES: 4 servings   **HANDS-ON TIME: 22 MIN.**
TOTAL TIME: 43 MIN.

Using spicy Italian sausage will add a bit of heat to these delectable savory treats.

5 oz. mild Italian bulk pork sausage	¼ tsp. crushed red pepper
1½ tsp. canola oil	1 (14.1-oz.) package refrigerated piecrusts
¼ cup chopped red bell pepper	½ cup (2 oz.) shredded part-skim mozzarella cheese
½ bunch fresh kale, washed, trimmed and cut into strips (about 1⅓ cups)	Parchment paper
1 cup refrigerated diced potato with onion	1 Tbsp. heavy cream
¼ tsp. table salt	2 Tbsp. finely shredded Parmesan cheese
¼ tsp. freshly ground black pepper	

1. Preheat oven to 400°. Cook sausage in hot oil in a large skillet over medium-high heat, 6 minutes or until meat crumbles and is no longer pink. Remove sausage from skillet using a slotted spoon, reserving drippings in skillet. Sauté bell pepper, kale, and potato mixture in hot drippings 6 minutes or until tender; add sausage. Remove from heat; stir in salt, black pepper, and crushed red pepper.

2. Unroll piecrusts on a lightly floured surface. Cut each piecrust in half. Spoon about ½ cup sausage mixture into center of each half of dough; top each with half of mozzarella cheese. Fold dough over filling to form triangles. Brush edges of dough with water. Press edges together with a fork to firmly seal. Place pies on a parchment paper-lined baking sheet. Cut small slits in top for steam to escape.

3. Brush tops of pies with cream, and sprinkle with Parmesan cheese.

4. Bake at 400° for 20 minutes or until golden. Serve warm or at room temperature, or cover pies until ready to serve.

* Note: Prepare pies through Step 2; freeze until firm. Store pies in a zip-top plastic freezer bag. To bake, preheat oven to 400°. Remove pies from freezer (do not thaw). Place pies on a parchment paper-lined baking sheet. Brush with cream and sprinkle with Parmesan cheese; bake as directed in recipe.

grocery guide:

❑ 1 (14-oz.) package mild Italian bulk pork sausage
❑ 1 red bell pepper
❑ 1 bunch fresh kale
❑ 1 (20-oz.) container refrigerated diced potato with onion
❑ Parchment paper
❑ 1 pt. heavy cream

Chicken Tetrazzini

Makes: 12 servings   **Hands-On Time: 20 min.**
Total Time: 55 min.

1	(16-oz.) package vermicelli	1	(8-oz.) container sour cream
½	cup chicken broth	1	(6-oz.) jar sliced mushrooms, drained
4	cups chopped cooked chicken breasts	½	cup (2 oz.) shredded Parmesan cheese
1	(10 ¾-oz.) can cream of mushroom soup	½	tsp. table salt
1	(10 ¾-oz.) can cream of chicken soup	1	tsp. black pepper
1	(10 ¾-oz.) can cream of celery soup	2	cups (8 oz.) shredded Cheddar cheese

1. Preheat oven to 350°.

2. Cook vermicelli according to package directions, stirring in chicken broth during last 5 minutes of cooking; drain.

3. Combine chicken and next 8 ingredients in a large bowl; add vermicelli, stirring well. Spoon mixture into 2 lightly greased 11- x 7-inch baking dishes. Sprinkle evenly with Cheddar cheese.

4. Bake, covered, at 350° for 30 minutes; uncover and bake 5 more minutes or until casserole is bubbly and cheese is melted.

 * Note: To make ahead, freeze an unbaked casserole up to 1 month, if desired. Thaw overnight in refrigerator. Let stand at room temperature 30 minutes, and bake as directed.

grocery guide:
❏ 1 (16-oz.) package vermicelli

Easy Chicken and Dumplings

**MAKES: 4 TO 6 SERVINGS   HANDS-ON TIME: 30 MIN.
TOTAL TIME: 40 MIN.**

1   (32-oz.) container reduced-
     sodium chicken broth
3   cups shredded cooked
     chicken
1   (10 ¾-oz.) can reduced-fat
     cream of chicken soup

¼   tsp. poultry seasoning
1   (10.2-oz.) can refrigerated
     jumbo buttermilk biscuits
2   carrots, diced
3   celery ribs, diced

1. Bring first 4 ingredients to a boil in a Dutch oven over medium-high heat. Cover, reduce heat to low, and simmer, stirring occasionally, 5 minutes. Increase heat to medium-high; return to a low boil.

2. Place biscuits on a lightly floured surface. Roll or pat each biscuit to ⅛-inch thickness; cut into ½-inch-wide strips.

3. Drop strips, 1 at a time, into boiling broth mixture. Add carrots and celery. Cover, reduce heat to low, and simmer 15 to 20 minutes, stirring occasionally to prevent dumplings from sticking.

   * Note: To make ahead, freeze up to 1 month in a zip-top plastic freezer bag. To reheat, heat frozen chicken and dumplings to simmer over low heat, stirring occasionally.

grocery guide:

❏ 1 (0.65-oz.) jar poultry
    seasoning
❏ 1 (10.2-oz.) can refrigerated
    jumbo buttermilk biscuits
❏ 1 bunch carrots
❏ 1 bunch celery ribs

Anytime Chicken and Dressing

MAKES: 6 SERVINGS   **HANDS-ON TIME: 30 MIN.**
TOTAL TIME: 1 HOUR, 30 MIN.

¼ cup butter
7 green onions, chopped
2 celery ribs, chopped
10 cornbread muffins, crumbled (about 3 ½ cups)
½ (16-oz.) package herb-seasoned stuffing mix
5 cups chicken broth
1 ½ cups chopped cooked chicken
2 large eggs, lightly beaten
½ tsp. poultry seasoning

1. Preheat oven to 350°. Melt butter in a large skillet over medium heat; add green onions and celery, and sauté 5 minutes or until tender.

2. Combine cornbread and remaining ingredients in a large bowl; add sautéed vegetable mixture, stirring well. Spoon dressing into a lightly greased 13- x 9-inch baking dish.

3. Bake, uncovered, at 350° for 45 minutes or until lightly browned.

  * Note: To make ahead, cover baking dish tightly with heavy-duty aluminum foil before baking; label and freeze up to 2 months. To heat, let casserole thaw overnight in fridge. Uncover and bake as directed.

grocery guide:

- ❏ 2 bunches green onions
- ❏ 1 bunch celery ribs
- ❏ 10 cornbread muffins
- ❏ 1 (16-oz.) package herb-seasoned stuffing mix
- ❏ 1 (0.65-oz.) jar poultry seasoning

Chicken 'n' Spinach Pasta Bake

MAKES: 4 TO 6 SERVINGS   HANDS-ON TIME: 15 MIN.
TOTAL TIME: 1 HOUR, 15 MIN.

8 oz. uncooked rigatoni pasta	1 (14 ½-oz.) can Italian-style diced tomatoes
1 Tbsp. olive oil	1 (8-oz.) container chive-and-onion cream cheese
1 cup finely chopped onion (about 1 medium)	½ tsp. table salt
1 (10-oz.) package frozen chopped spinach, thawed	½ tsp. black pepper
3 cups cubed cooked chicken breasts	1 ½ cups (6 oz.) shredded mozzarella cheese

1. Preheat oven to 375°.

2. Prepare rigatoni according to package directions.

3. Meanwhile, spread oil on bottom of an 11- x 7-inch baking dish; add onion in a single layer.

4. Bake at 375° for 15 minutes or just until tender. Transfer onion to a large bowl, and set aside.

5. Drain chopped spinach well, pressing between paper towels.

6. Add rigatoni, spinach, chicken, and next 4 ingredients to onion mixture. Spoon mixture into an 11- x 7-inch baking dish, and sprinkle evenly with shredded mozzarella cheese.

7. Bake, covered, at 375° for 30 minutes; uncover and bake 15 more minutes or until bubbly.

* Note: To make ahead, freeze the casserole up to 1 month. To reheat, thaw in the refrigerator overnight and bake as directed.

grocery guide:

- ❏ 1 (16-oz.) package uncooked rigatoni
- ❏ 1 medium onion
- ❏ 1 (10-oz.) package frozen chopped spinach
- ❏ 1 (8-oz.) container chive-and-onion cream cheese

Turkey-Mushroom Lasagna

MAKES: 8 servings   **HANDS-ON TIME: 25 MIN.**
TOTAL TIME: 1 HOUR, 45 MIN.

1 lb. ground Italian turkey sausage, casings removed	2 Tbsp. dried parsley flakes
1 (26-oz.) jar tomato-and-basil pasta sauce	1 Tbsp. grated Parmesan cheese
1 (8-oz.) can sliced mushrooms, drained	¼ tsp. table salt
1 (32-oz.) container reduced-fat ricotta cheese	10 uncooked lasagna noodles
1 large egg, lightly beaten	4 cups (16 oz.) shredded mozzarella cheese
	Garnish: chopped fresh basil

1. Preheat oven to 375°.

2. Brown turkey sausage in a lightly greased large nonstick skillet over medium-high heat, stirring occasionally, 8 to 10 minutes or until meat crumbles and is no longer pink. Drain sausage, and return to skillet. Stir in pasta sauce and mushrooms; set aside.

3. Stir together ricotta cheese and next 4 ingredients in a large bowl until blended.

4. Layer 5 lasagna noodles lengthwise in a lightly greased 13- x 9-inch baking dish; top with half of the turkey mixture, half of the ricotta cheese mixture, and 2 cups shredded mozzarella cheese. Repeat layers once.

5. Bake, covered, at 375° for 55 minutes; uncover and bake 10 to 15 more minutes or until lasagna is bubbly. Let stand 10 minutes before serving.

* Note: To make ahead, freeze unbaked lasagna up to 3 months. To prepare, thaw in refrigerator overnight. Let stand 30 minutes; bake as directed.

grocery guide:

❑ 1 lb. ground Italian turkey sausage
❑ 1 (32-oz.) container low-fat ricotta cheese
❑ 1 (1.2-oz.) container dried parsley flakes
❑ 1 (10-oz.) package lasagna noodles
❑ Optional: 1 bunch fresh basil

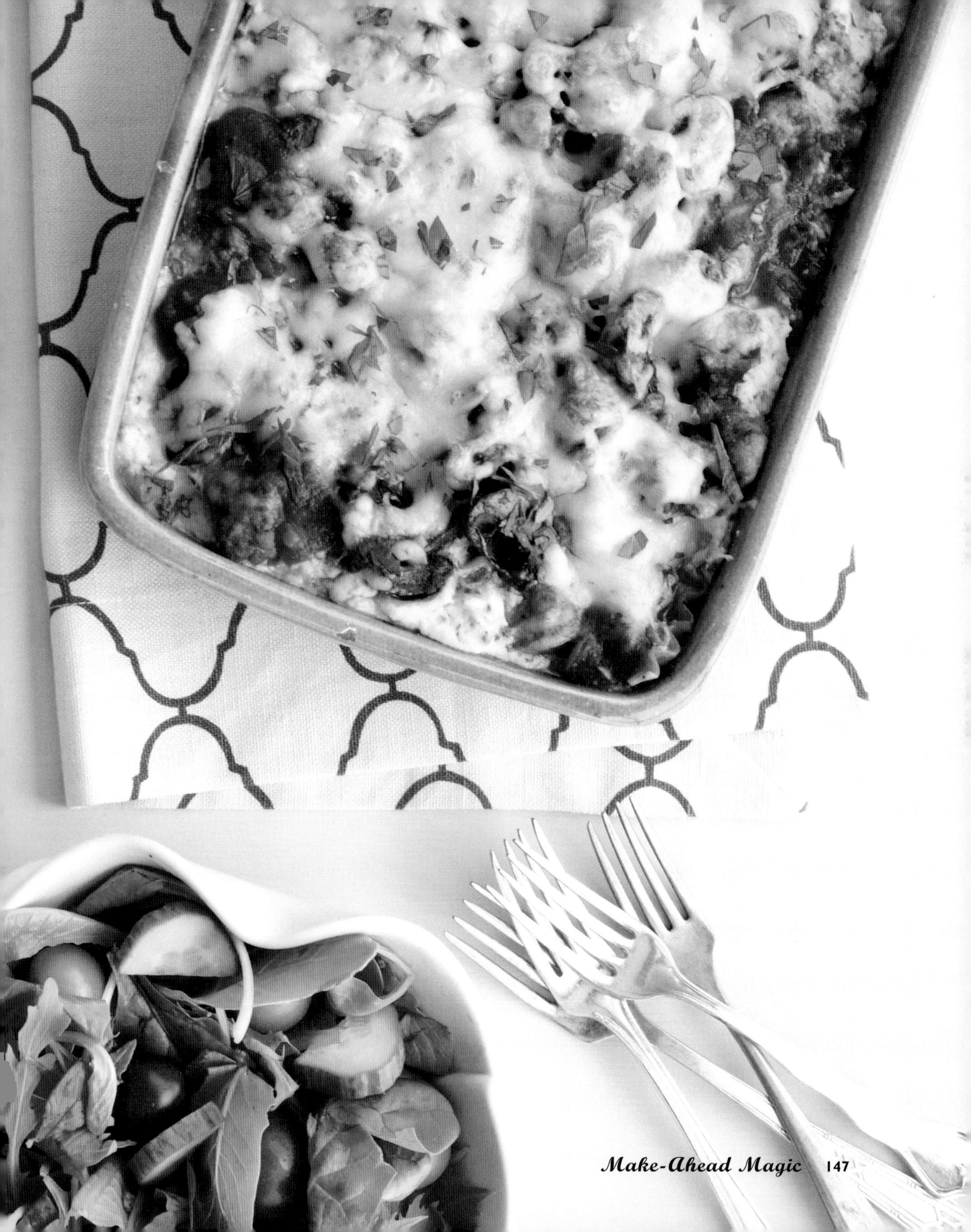

What's for Supper

Cajun Shrimp Casserole

MAKES: 6 SERVINGS   **HANDS-ON TIME: 46 MIN.**
TOTAL TIME: 1 HOUR, 6 MIN.

2	lb. unpeeled, large raw shrimp	2	cups fresh or frozen cut okra
¼	cup butter	1	Tbsp. fresh lemon juice
1	small red onion, chopped*	1½	tsp. table salt
½	cup chopped red bell pepper*	3	cups cooked long-grain rice
½	cup chopped yellow bell pepper*	1	(10 ¾-oz.) can cream of shrimp soup**
½	cup chopped green bell pepper*	½	cup dry white wine
4	garlic cloves, minced	1	Tbsp. soy sauce
		½	tsp. ground red pepper
		¼	cup grated Parmesan cheese

1. Preheat oven to 350°.

2. Peel shrimp; devein, if desired.

3. Melt butter in a large skillet over medium-high heat. Add onion and next 3 ingredients; sauté 7 minutes or until tender. Add garlic, and sauté 1 minute. Stir in okra, lemon juice, and salt; sauté 5 minutes. Add shrimp, and cook 3 minutes or until shrimp turn pink. Stir in rice and next 4 ingredients until blended. Pour into a lightly greased 11- x 7-inch baking dish. Sprinkle evenly with Parmesan cheese.

4. Bake at 350° for 15 to 20 minutes or until casserole is bubbly and cheese is lightly browned.

  * 1 (10-oz.) package frozen onions and peppers may be substituted for fresh onion and bell peppers.

  ** 1 (10 ¾-oz.) can cream of mushroom soup may be substituted for cream of shrimp soup.

  *** Note: Unbaked casserole may be made one day in advance. Cover and refrigerate. Let stand at room temperature 30 minutes before baking as directed. To freeze unbaked casserole, prepare as directed, omitting Parmesan cheese. Cover tightly, and freeze. Let stand at room temperature 30 minutes before baking. Bake, covered, at 350° for 50 minutes. Uncover, sprinkle evenly with Parmesan cheese, and bake 10 more minutes or until cheese is lightly browned.

grocery guide:

- ❏ 2 lb. unpeeled, large raw shrimp
- ❏ 1 small red onion
- ❏ 1 red bell pepper
- ❏ 1 yellow bell pepper
- ❏ 1 green bell pepper
- ❏ 1 small garlic bulb
- ❏ 1 (16-oz.) package fresh or frozen sliced okra
- ❏ 1 lemon
- ❏ 1 (10 ¾ oz.) can cream of shrimp soup

Quick Crawfish Étouffée

MAKES: 6 SERVINGS   **HANDS-ON TIME: 41 MIN.**
TOTAL TIME: 41 MIN.

1 cup uncooked long-grain rice	1 (14-oz.) can chicken broth
¼ cup butter	1 Tbsp. salt-free Cajun seasoning
1 large onion, chopped	
1 green bell pepper, chopped	⅛ to ¼ tsp. ground red pepper
4 celery ribs, chopped (about 1 cup)	1 lb. frozen cooked, peeled crawfish tails, thawed and drained
4 garlic cloves, minced	
1 (10 ¾-oz.) can cream of mushroom soup	¼ cup chopped green onions
	3 Tbsp. chopped fresh parsley

1. Prepare rice according to package directions.

2. Melt butter in a large cast-iron skillet or Dutch oven over medium heat. Add onion and next 3 ingredients; cook, stirring constantly, 8 minutes.

3. Stir together soup and chicken broth. Add to vegetable mixture. Stir in Cajun seasoning and ground red pepper.

4. Cook over medium-low heat 10 minutes, stirring occasionally. Stir in crawfish, green onions, and parsley; cook 3 minutes or until hot. Serve over rice.

  * Note: To make ahead, divide étouffée into 3 (1-qt.) zip-top plastic freezer bags. Freeze up to 1 month. To reheat, thaw in refrigerator over-night. Remove from freezer bag, and cook in a saucepan over medium-low heat, stirring until thoroughly heated. Each bag contains about 2 servings.

Vanessa's Savvy Secret:
Purchase frozen cooked, peeled crawfish tails in the freezer section of your grocery store. I prefer Louisiana crawfish tails rather than Chinese ones. To mail order, visit cajuncrawfish.com.

grocery guide:

❑ 1 large onion
❑ 1 green bell pepper
❑ 1 bunch celery ribs
❑ 1 small garlic bulb
❑ 1 lb. frozen cooked, peeled crawfish tails
❑ 1 bunch green onions
❑ 1 bunch fresh parsley

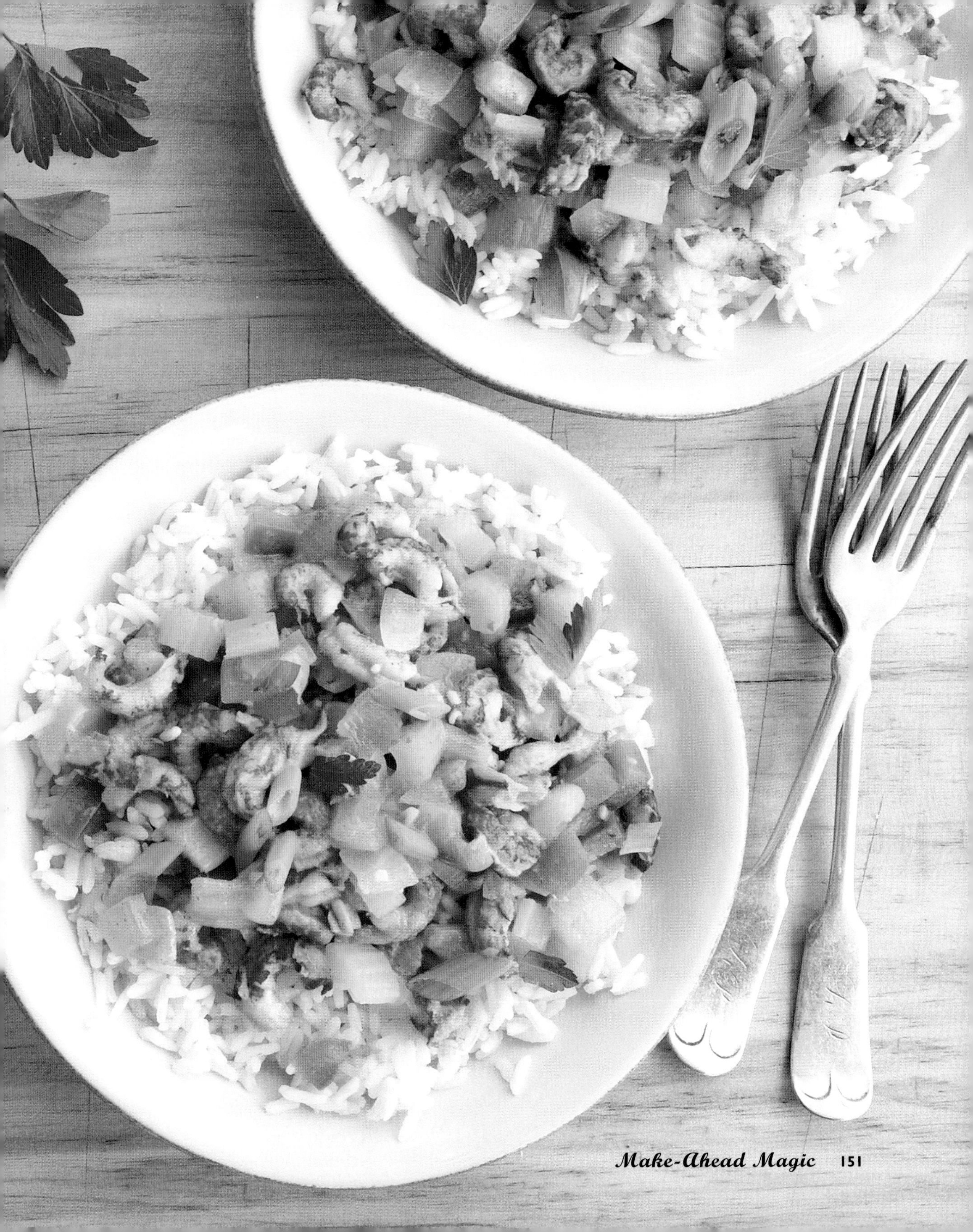

Artichoke, Asparagus, and Goat Cheese Strata

Makes: 6 servings   Hands-On Time: 10 min.
Total Time: 45 min., plus 1 day for soaking

4	large eggs	½	lb. fresh asparagus
2	cups milk	1	small onion, chopped
½	cup (2 oz.) freshly grated Parmesan cheese	1	(14-oz.) can quartered artichoke hearts, drained
½	tsp. table salt	6	ounces French bread, cut into 1-inch cubes (6 cups)
½	tsp. freshly ground black pepper	8	oz. crumbled goat cheese
½	tsp. dried oregano	½	cup halved grape tomatoes
2	garlic cloves, minced		

1. Whisk eggs in a large bowl until smooth. Whisk in milk and next 5 ingredients. Snap off and discard tough ends of asparagus. Cut asparagus into 1-inch pieces. Stir in asparagus, onion, and artichoke hearts. Add bread, stirring gently to coat. Cover and chill 24 hours.

2. Preheat oven to 375°. Spoon half of bread mixture into a lightly greased 2-quart baking dish. Sprinkle with half of goat cheese. Top with remaining bread mixture, remaining goat cheese, and tomatoes.

3. Bake, uncovered, at 375° for 35 minutes or until browned and set.

  * Note: To make ahead, prepare through Step 2. Cover and chill up to 24 hours. Bake time will increase by about 10 minutes.

grocery guide:

- ❑ 1 garlic bulb
- ❑ 1 bunch fresh asparagus
- ❑ 1 small onion
- ❑ 1 (16-oz.) French bread loaf
- ❑ 2 (4-oz.) packages crumbled goat cheese
- ❑ 1 pt. grape tomatoes

Chunky Vegetable Soup,

MAKES: 8 servings　　　**HANDS-ON TIME: 25 MIN.**
TOTAL TIME: 45 MIN.

2	lb. ground chuck	1	(15-oz.) can sweet peas with mushrooms and pearl onions, drained and rinsed
1	small sweet onion, chopped		
1	tsp. table salt		
½	tsp. black pepper	2	(26-oz.) jars tomato, herbs, and spices pasta sauce
3	(14-oz.) cans reduced-sodium beef broth		
		1	(14 ½-oz.) can diced tomatoes with sweet onion
3	(29-oz.) cans mixed vegetables with potatoes, drained and rinsed		
			Garnish: chopped fresh basil
3	(14 ½-oz.) cans diced new potatoes, drained and rinsed		

grocery guide:

- ❏ 2 lb. ground chuck
- ❏ 1 small sweet onion
- ❏ 3 (29-oz.) cans mixed vegetables with potatoes
- ❏ 3 (14 ½-oz.) cans diced new potatoes
- ❏ 1 (15-oz.) can sweet peas with mushrooms and pearl onions
- ❏ Optional: 1 bunch fresh basil

1. Brown ground chuck and onion, in batches, in a large Dutch oven over medium-high heat, stirring 5 to 8 minutes or until meat crumbles and is no longer pink. Drain well, and return to Dutch oven. Stir in salt, black pepper, and beef broth; bring to a boil.

2. Stir in mixed vegetables and next 4 ingredients. Bring to a boil; cover, reduce heat, and simmer at least 20 minutes or until thoroughly heated.

*** Note:** To make ahead, freeze in meal-size portions in large zip-top plastic freezer bags. Fold top edge down, and place in a large glass measuring cup to stabilize the bag while filling; freeze up to 1 month. To reheat, thaw soup in fridge overnight, and simmer over low heat, stirring occasionally.

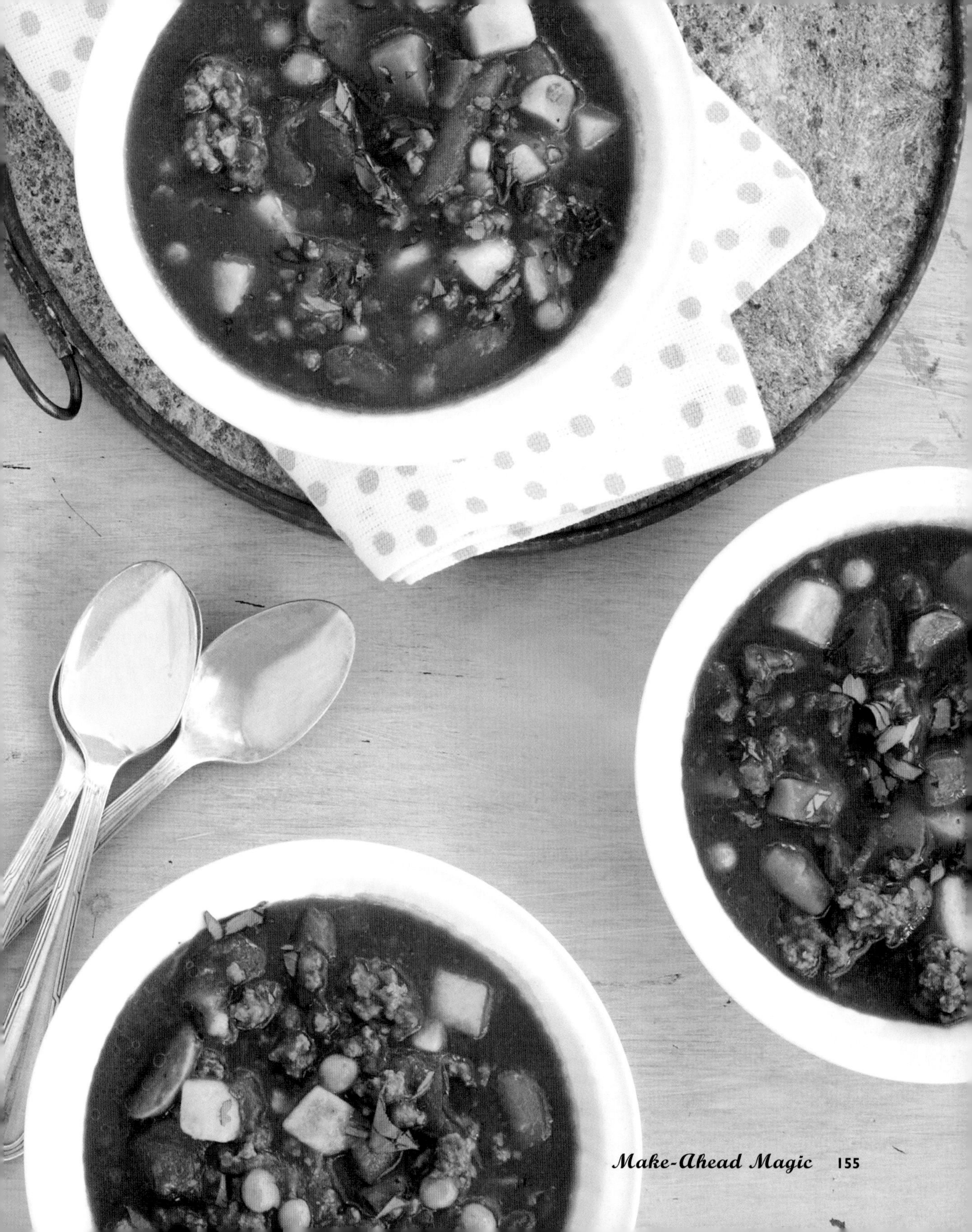

Asian Noodle Salad

MAKES: 6 TO 8 SERVINGS   **HANDS-ON TIME: 10 MIN.**
TOTAL TIME: 20 MIN.

To make ahead, toss together all ingredients except cabbage. Cover and chill up to 24 hours. Toss in cabbage and cilantro and sprinkle with peanuts just before serving.

1	(8-oz.) package wide lo-mein noodles	2	cups shredded deli-roasted chicken
6	Tbsp. soy sauce	1	cup thinly sliced napa cabbage
6	Tbsp. peanut oil	½	cup matchstick carrots
¼	cup seasoned rice vinegar	4	green onions, thinly sliced
2	Tbsp. fresh lime juice	½	red bell pepper, thinly sliced
2	Tbsp. dark sesame oil	⅓	cup loosely packed fresh cilantro leaves
2	Tbsp. hoisin sauce		
4	tsp. grated fresh ginger	¼	cup chopped unsalted dry-roasted peanuts
2	tsp. Asian hot chili sauce (such as Sriracha)		

1. Cook noodles according to package directions. Plunge noodles into ice water for 10 minutes to stop the cooking process; drain.

2. Whisk together soy sauce and next 7 ingredients in a large bowl. Add noodles, chicken, and next 4 ingredients, and toss well. Toss with cilantro just before serving; sprinkle with peanuts.

Stretch Your Budget: This recipe calls for 2 cups of deli-roasted chicken, and a whole deli-roasted chicken typically provides 3 cups of chicken. Use the extra cup of chicken to make salads or sandwiches for lunch the next day.

grocery guide:

- ❑ 1 (8-oz.) package wide lo-mein noodles
- ❑ 1 (12-oz.) bottle seasoned rice vinegar
- ❑ 1 lime
- ❑ 1 (6.2-oz.) jar dark sesame oil
- ❑ 1 (7-oz.) jar hoisin sauce
- ❑ Fresh ginger
- ❑ 1 (16-oz.) bottle Asian hot chili sauce (such as Sriracha)
- ❑ 1 deli-roasted chicken
- ❑ 1 head napa cabbage
- ❑ 1 (16-oz.) package matchstick carrots
- ❑ 1 bunch green onions
- ❑ 1 red bell pepper
- ❑ 1 bunch fresh cilantro
- ❑ 1 can chopped unsalted dry-roasted peanuts

breakfast
for dinner

Eggs, bacon, and all your morning favorites make a fast and fun choice for dinner.

Asparagus Frittata

MAKES: 6 SERVINGS   **HANDS-ON TIME: 30 MIN.**
TOTAL TIME: 30 MIN.

1	lb. fresh thin asparagus
2	Tbsp. butter
1	small onion, coarsely chopped
1	garlic clove, minced
12	large eggs
½	cup sour cream
¾	tsp. freshly ground black pepper
½	tsp. kosher salt
1	cup (4 oz.) shredded Gouda cheese
¼	cup freshly grated Parmesan cheese

Garnish: small fresh basil leaves

1. Preheat oven to 350° with oven rack 6 inches from top of heat source. Snap off and discard tough ends of asparagus. Cut asparagus diagonally into 1-inch pieces. Melt butter in a 10-inch ovenproof skillet over medium-high heat; add onion, and sauté 3 to 4 minutes or until onion is tender. Add asparagus; sauté 3 to 4 minutes or until tender. Add garlic, and sauté 1 minute.

2. Whisk together eggs and next 3 ingredients until well blended. Stir in ¾ cup Gouda cheese. Fold egg mixture into vegetable mixture in skillet. Cook, stirring occasionally, 2 to 3 minutes or until almost set. Sprinkle with Parmesan cheese and remaining ¼ cup Gouda cheese.

3. Bake at 350° for 5 minutes or until set. Increase oven temperature to broil, and broil 3 to 4 minutes or until golden brown.

Kid Flip: Substitute smoked Cheddar for the Gouda cheese if your kids would prefer it.

grocery guide:

❏ 1 lb. fresh thin asparagus
❏ 1 small onion
❏ 1 small garlic bulb
❏ 1 (4-oz.) package shredded Gouda cheese
❏ Optional: 1 bunch fresh basil

Fried Egg Sandwiches

MAKES: 4 SERVINGS　　**HANDS-ON TIME: 25 MIN.**
TOTAL TIME: 27 MIN.

These open-faced egg sandwiches are true comfort-food goodness with layers of pancetta, arugula, and fried eggs on top of challah bread—not to mention the savory hollandaise sauce spooned on top.

4	(½-inch-thick) challah bread slices	¼	cup thinly sliced red onion
2	Tbsp. butter, melted	3	tsp. extra virgin olive oil, divided
1	(0.9-oz.) envelope hollandaise sauce mix	4	large eggs
¼	tsp. lemon zest	¼	tsp. kosher salt
1½	tsp. fresh lemon juice, divided	¼	tsp. freshly ground black pepper
2	cups loosely packed arugula	12	thin pancetta slices, cooked
½	cup loosely packed fresh flat-leaf parsley leaves	2	Tbsp. chopped sun-dried tomatoes

1. Preheat broiler with oven rack 5 to 6 inches from heat. Brush both sides of bread with butter; place on an aluminum foil-lined broiler pan. Broil 1 to 2 minutes on each side or until lightly toasted.

2. Prepare hollandaise sauce according to package directions; stir in zest and ½ tsp. lemon juice. Keep warm.

3. Toss together arugula, parsley, onion, 2 tsp. oil, and remaining 1 tsp. lemon juice.

4. Heat remaining 1 tsp. oil in a large nonstick skillet over medium heat. Gently break eggs into hot skillet; sprinkle with salt and black pepper. Cook 2 to 3 minutes on each side or to desired degree of doneness.

5. Top bread slices with arugula mixture, pancetta slices, and fried eggs. Spoon hollandaise sauce over each egg, and sprinkle with tomatoes. Serve immediately.

grocery guide:

- ❏ 1 loaf challah bread
- ❏ 1 (0.9-oz.) envelope hollandaise sauce mix
- ❏ 1 lemon
- ❏ 1 (5-oz.) package arugula
- ❏ 1 bunch fresh flat-leaf parsley
- ❏ 1 small red onion
- ❏ 12 thin pancetta slices
- ❏ 1 (7.5-oz.) jar sun-dried tomatoes

Speedy Huevos Rancheros

MAKES: 4 SERVINGS   **HANDS-ON TIME: 29 MIN.**
TOTAL TIME: 29 MIN.

1 cup chopped onion	8 large eggs
1 cup chopped green, yellow, and red bell peppers	½ cup refried beans, warmed
1 tsp. minced garlic	8 (6-inch) fajita-size corn or flour tortillas, warmed
3 Tbsp. vegetable oil, divided	¾ cup (6 oz.) shredded pepper Jack cheese
2 Tbsp. chopped fresh cilantro	Hot sauce (optional)
½ tsp. table salt, divided	Garnish: additional fresh cilantro
1 (14 ½-oz.) can diced zesty chili-style tomatoes	

1. Sauté first 3 ingredients in 1 Tbsp. hot oil in a nonstick skillet over medium-high heat 5 minutes or until crisp-tender. Stir in 2 Tbsp. cilantro, ¼ tsp. salt, and tomatoes. Bring to a boil; reduce heat, and simmer, uncovered, 3 minutes or until thickened.

2. Meanwhile, heat 1 Tbsp. oil in a medium nonstick skillet over medium heat. Gently break 4 eggs into hot skillet; sprinkle with ⅛ tsp. salt. Cook, covered, 2 to 3 minutes or to desired degree of doneness. Transfer eggs to a plate. Repeat procedure with remaining 1 Tbsp. oil, remaining 4 eggs, and remaining ⅛ tsp. salt.

3. Spread refried beans over tortillas; top with tomato sauce. Top each serving with 1 egg, and sprinkle with cheese. Fold tortillas in half; serve immediately with hot sauce, if desired.

Make It Snappy: Omit homemade tomato sauce, and just use chunky salsa.

grocery guide:

- ❏ 1 medium onion
- ❏ 1 (8-oz.) container chopped green, yellow, and red bell peppers
- ❏ 1 small garlic bulb
- ❏ 1 bunch fresh cilantro
- ❏ 1 (14 ½-oz.) can diced zesty chili-style tomatoes
- ❏ 1 (16-oz.) can refried beans
- ❏ Hot sauce (optional)

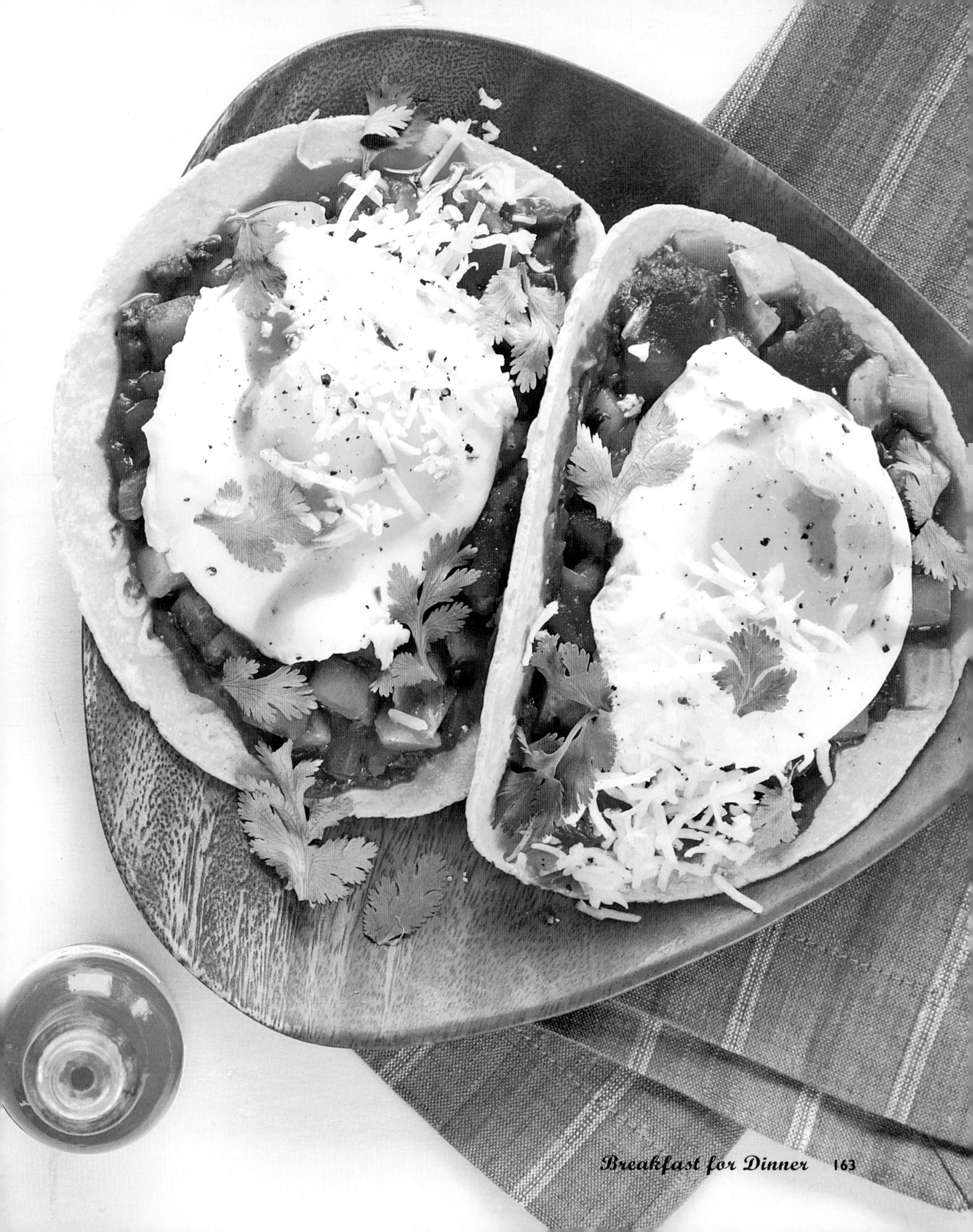

Cheddar Pancake Egg Wraps

MAKES: 4 SERVINGS **HANDS-ON TIME: 15 MIN.**
TOTAL TIME: 30 MIN.

1 cup all-purpose baking mix*	¼ tsp. freshly ground black pepper
¾ cup milk	2 green onions, finely chopped
1 large egg	4 bacon slices
½ cup (2 oz.) shredded sharp Cheddar cheese	Parchment paper
8 large eggs	Kitchen string
2 Tbsp. milk	Toppings: salsa, additional shredded sharp Cheddar cheese, sour cream
¼ tsp. table salt	

1. Whisk together first 3 ingredients in a medium bowl until blended. Stir in cheese.

2. Pour about ⅓ cup batter for each pancake, 1 at a time, onto a hot, lightly greased griddle or large nonstick skillet over medium heat, spreading to 6 inches. Cook pancakes 2 minutes or until tops are covered with bubbles and edges look dry and cooked; turn and cook 2 more minutes. (Keep pancakes warm in a 200° oven up to 30 minutes.)

3. Whisk together eggs, milk, and next 3 ingredients. Cook bacon in a large skillet over medium-high heat 2 to 3 minutes or until crisp; remove bacon, reserving 2 tsp. drippings in skillet. Crumble bacon. Add egg mixture to skillet, and cook over medium heat, without stirring, 1 to 2 minutes or until eggs begin to set on bottom. Gently draw cooked edges away from sides of skillet to form large pieces. Cook, stirring occasionally, 2 to 3 more minutes or until eggs are thickened and moist. (Do not overstir.)

4. Divide eggs and bacon equally among pancakes, spooning ingredients down center of each pancake. Roll up pancakes. Wrap in parchment paper, and tie with kitchen string. Serve immediately with desired toppings.

*We tested with Bisquick Original Pancake and Baking Mix.

grocery guide:
❏ 1 bunch green onions
❏ Kitchen string
❏ Parchment paper

Chicken, Egg, and Cheese Burritos

MAKES: 4 SERVINGS **HANDS-ON TIME: 12 MIN.**
TOTAL TIME: 12 MIN.

Pick up prepared chicken fingers from the deli of your local grocery store, and dinner will be ready in record time. If the chicken is salty, there's no need to add salt to your eggs.

8	large eggs	8	deli-fried chicken tenders,
¼	cup milk		cut into bite-size pieces
¼	tsp. table salt	¼	cup chopped green onions
¼	tsp. freshly ground black pepper	4	(10-inch) burrito-size flour
Dash of ground red pepper			tortillas
1	Tbsp. butter	Salsa	
1½	cups (6 oz.) shredded sharp	Sour cream	
	Cheddar cheese		

1. Whisk together first 5 ingredients in a large bowl.

2. Melt butter in a large nonstick skillet over medium heat. Add egg mixture, and cook, without stirring, 1 to 1½ minutes or until eggs begin to set on bottom. Sprinkle with cheese. Gently draw cooked edges away from sides of skillet to form large pieces. Cook, stirring occasionally, 30 seconds or until eggs are thickened and moist. (Do not overstir.)

3. Remove from heat. Gently stir in chicken and green onions. Spoon about 1½ cups egg mixture just below center of each tortilla. Fold opposite sides of tortilla over filling, and roll up. Serve with salsa and sour cream.

Gourmet Flip: Pick up a rotisserie chicken from the deli instead of the chicken fingers to use in this recipe.

grocery guide:
- ❏ 8 deli-fried chicken tenders
- ❏ 1 bunch green onions
- ❏ 1 (12-oz.) jar salsa

Mini Sausage-and-Egg Casseroles

MAKES: 10 SERVINGS **HANDS-ON TIME: 20 MIN.**
TOTAL TIME: 45 MIN.

8	(1½-oz.) sourdough bread slices, cut into ½-inch cubes	1	Tbsp. Dijon mustard
1	(12-oz.) package fully-cooked pork sausage patties, chopped	½	cup buttermilk
2½	cups 2% reduced-fat milk	1	(10¾-oz.) can cream of mushroom soup
4	large eggs	1	cup (4 oz.) shredded sharp Cheddar cheese

1. Preheat oven to 350°.

2. Divide bread cubes evenly among 10 (8- to 10-oz.) ovenproof coffee mugs coated with cooking spray, placing in bottom of mugs. Top with sausage. Whisk together 2½ cups milk, eggs, and Dijon mustard. Pour over bread mixture in mugs.

3. Whisk together buttermilk and cream of mushroom soup. Spoon over bread mixture in mugs; sprinkle with Cheddar cheese. Place coffee mugs on a baking sheet.

4. Bake at 350° for 25 to 30 minutes or until casseroles are set and puffed. Serve immediately.

   * Note: Mugs (or ramekins) of unbaked casserole can be covered with plastic wrap, then foil, and frozen up to 1 month. Thaw overnight in the refrigerator. Bake as directed in Step 4.

Sausage-and-Egg Casserole:
Omit ramekins. Arrange bread in 2 lightly greased 8-inch square baking dishes or 1 lightly greased 13- x 9-inch baking dish. Proceed as directed, increasing bake time to 1 hour or until casserole is set.

grocery guide:
❏ 1 sourdough bread loaf
❏ 1 (12-oz.) package fully-cooked pork patties
❏ 1 pt. buttermilk

Creamy Egg Strata

MAKES: 8 TO 10 SERVINGS   HANDS-ON TIME: 35 MIN.
TOTAL TIME: 10 HOURS, 10 MIN.

½	(16-oz.) French bread loaf, cubed (about 5 cups)	1 ½	cups chicken broth
6	Tbsp. butter, divided	¾	cup dry white wine
2	cups (8 oz.) shredded Swiss cheese	½	tsp. table salt
½	cup freshly grated Parmesan cheese	½	tsp. freshly ground black pepper
⅓	cup chopped onion	¼	tsp. ground nutmeg
1	tsp. minced garlic	½	cup sour cream
3	Tbsp. all-purpose flour	8	large eggs, lightly beaten

Garnish: chopped fresh chives

1. Place bread cubes in a well-buttered 13- x 9-inch baking dish. Melt 3 Tbsp. butter, and drizzle over bread cubes. Sprinkle with cheeses.

2. Melt remaining 3 Tbsp. butter in a medium saucepan over medium heat; add onion and garlic. Sauté 2 to 3 minutes or until tender. Whisk in flour until smooth; cook, whisking constantly, 2 to 3 minutes or until lightly browned. Whisk in broth and next 4 ingredients until blended. Bring mixture to a boil; reduce heat to medium-low, and simmer, stirring occasionally, 15 minutes or until thickened. Remove from heat. Stir in sour cream. Add salt and pepper to taste.

3. Gradually whisk about one-fourth of hot sour cream mixture into eggs; add egg mixture to remaining sour cream mixture, whisking constantly. Pour mixture over cheese in baking dish. Cover with plastic wrap, and chill 8 to 24 hours.

4. Let strata stand at room temperature 1 hour. Preheat oven to 350°. Remove plastic wrap, and bake 30 minutes or until set. Serve immediately.

Make It Snappy: To chop the fresh chives even faster, use a rubber band to hold them together while you chop.

grocery guide:

❑ 1 French bread loaf
❑ 1 onion
❑ Optional: 1 bunch fresh chives

Sausage-and-Pepper Omelets

MAKES: 4 servings **HANDS-ON TIME: 20 MIN.**
TOTAL TIME: 20 MIN.

1	tsp. olive oil	8	large eggs
¾	lb. smoked sausage, chopped (2 ⅔ cups)	¼	tsp. table salt
1	(8-oz.) container refrigerated chopped tri-colored bell pepper	¼	tsp. freshly ground black pepper
2	Tbsp. chopped fresh parsley	4	tsp. butter, divided
		1	cup (4 oz.) shredded sharp Cheddar cheese

1. Heat oil in an 8-inch nonstick skillet over medium-high heat. Add sausage and bell pepper; sauté 5 minutes or until sausage is browned and vegetables are tender. Stir in parsley. Remove sausage mixture from pan. Wipe skillet clean with paper towels.

2. Whisk together eggs, salt, and black pepper.

3. Melt 1 tsp. butter in same skillet over medium heat. Pour ½ cup egg mixture into skillet. As egg mixture starts to cook, gently lift edges of omelet with a spatula, and tilt pan so uncooked portion flows underneath. Cook, uncovered, 1 to 2 minutes or until almost set.

4. Sprinkle 1 side of omelet with ¼ cup cheese and ⅔ cup reserved sausage mixture. Cook 1 to 2 minutes or until cheese begins to melt. Slide filled side of omelet onto a plate, flipping remaining side of omelet over filling. Repeat procedure 3 times with remaining butter, egg mixture, cheese, and sausage mixture. Serve immediately.

grocery guide:

❑ ¾ lb. smoked sausage
❑ 1 (8-oz.) container refrigerated chopped tri-colored bell pepper
❑ 1 bunch fresh parsley

Grits-and-Greens Breakfast Bake

MAKES: 8 servings   **HANDS-ON TIME: 25 min.**
TOTAL TIME: 2 hours, 7 min.

1	tsp. table salt	¼	tsp. ground red pepper
1 ½	cups uncooked quick-cooking grits	2	large eggs (not separated)
1	cup (4 oz.) shredded white Cheddar cheese	3	cups Simple Collard Greens, drained
3	Tbsp. butter	8	large eggs (not separated)
½	cup half-and-half		Hot sauce (optional)
¼	tsp. freshly ground black pepper		

1. Preheat oven to 375°. Bring salt and 4 cups water to a boil in a large saucepan over medium-high heat; gradually whisk in grits. Reduce heat to medium, and cook, whisking often, 5 to 7 minutes or until thickened. Remove from heat, and stir in cheese and butter.

2. Whisk together half-and-half, next 2 ingredients, and 2 eggs in a medium bowl. Stir half-and-half mixture into grits mixture. Stir in Simple Collard Greens. Pour mixture into a lightly greased 13- x 9-inch baking dish.

3. Bake at 375° for 25 to 30 minutes or until set. Remove from oven.

4. Make 8 indentations in grits mixture with back of a large spoon. Break remaining 8 eggs, 1 at a time, and slip 1 egg into each indentation. Bake 12 to 14 minutes or until eggs are cooked to desired degree of doneness. Cover loosely with aluminum foil, and let stand 10 minutes. Serve with hot sauce, if desired.

grocery guide:

- ❑ 1 pt. half-and-half
- ❑ 1 medium-size sweet onion
- ❑ 1 (16-oz.) package fresh collard greens

Simple Collard Greens

MAKES: 3 CUPS   HANDS-ON TIME: 20 MIN.
TOTAL TIME: 50 MIN.

½ medium-size sweet onion, chopped	1 (16-oz.) package fresh collard greens, washed, trimmed, and chopped
2 Tbsp. olive oil	1½ tsp. table salt

Cook onion in hot oil in a large Dutch oven over medium heat, stirring occasionally, 10 minutes or until tender. Add collard greens, salt, and 3 cups water. Bring to a boil; reduce heat, and simmer 30 minutes or until tender.

Hash Brown-and-Bacon Casserole

**MAKES: 8 TO 10 SERVINGS   HANDS-ON TIME: 20 MIN.
TOTAL TIME: 1 HOUR**

1	(10 ¾-oz.) can cream of chicken soup	½	cup chopped green onions
1	(8-oz.) container sour cream	1	(30-oz.) package frozen shredded hash browns, thawed
1	tsp. table salt		
¼	tsp. ground red pepper	2	cups cornflakes cereal, crushed
½	cup butter, melted and divided		
2	cups (8 oz.) shredded Monterey Jack cheese	8	cooked bacon slices, crumbled

1. Preheat oven to 350°. Stir together first 4 ingredients and ¼ cup butter in a large bowl until smooth. Stir in cheese and next 2 ingredients. Spoon potato mixture into a lightly greased 13- x 9-inch baking dish.

2. Toss together cornflakes, crumbled bacon, and remaining ¼ cup butter; sprinkle over potato mixture. Bake at 350° for 30 minutes or until bubbly and brown. Let stand 10 minutes before serving.

grocery guide:

- ❏ 1 bunch green onions
- ❏ 1 (30-oz.) package frozen shredded hash browns
- ❏ 1 (24-oz.) package cornflakes cereal

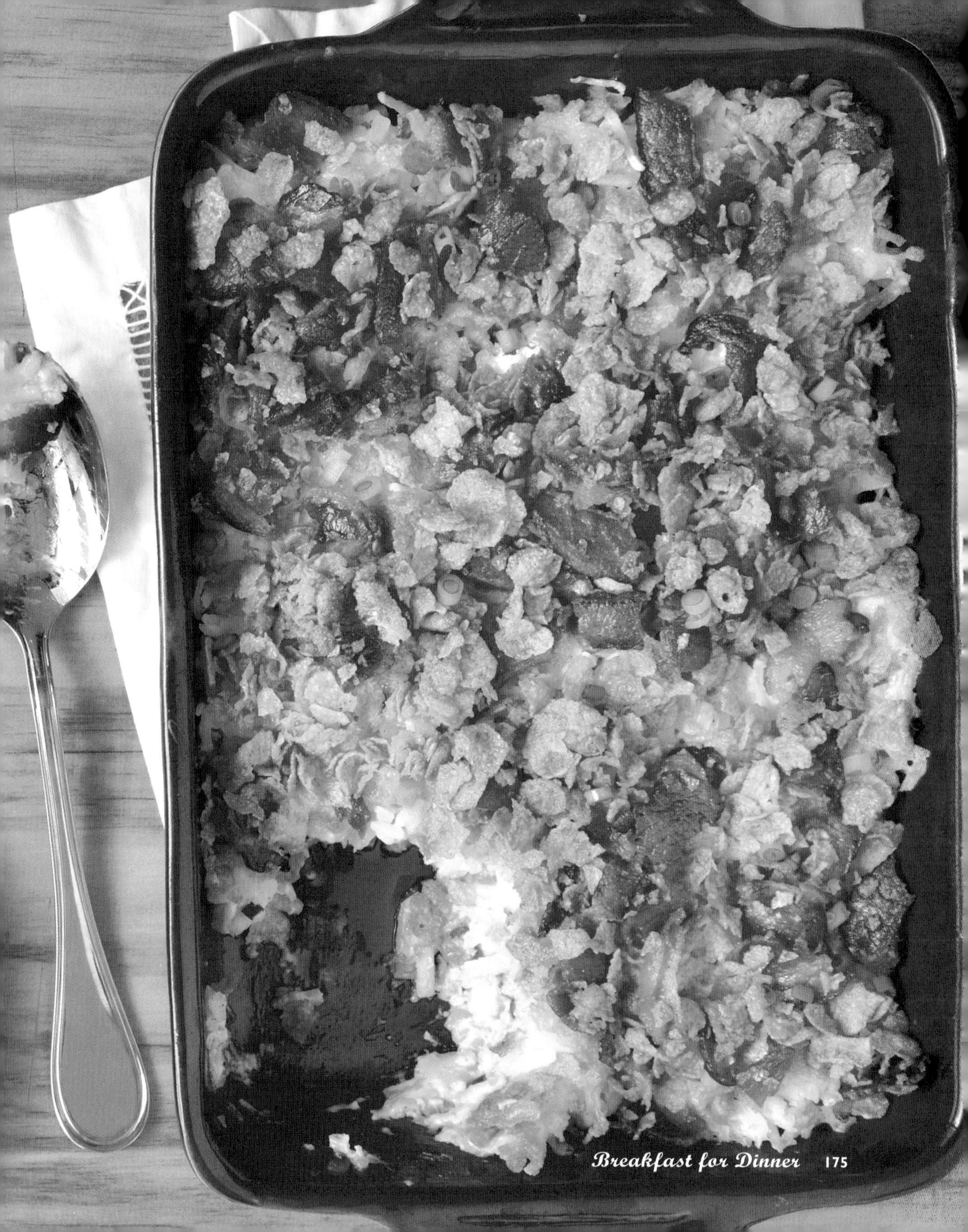

BBQ Pork-and-Grits Casserole

MAKES: 6 SERVINGS   **HANDS-ON TIME: 20 MIN.**
TOTAL TIME: 55 MIN.

Two Southern classics mingle in this mouthwatering casserole. Satisfy your taste buds with a spicy boost from your favorite barbecue sauce.

¾	lb. shredded barbecued pork without sauce	¼	cup butter
½	cup bottled barbecue sauce	1	large egg
4	cups milk	1	cup (4 oz.) extra-sharp white Cheddar cheese, shredded
1	cup uncooked quick-cooking grits	¼	cup chopped green onions
½	tsp. table salt		Additional barbecue sauce (optional)

1. Preheat oven to 350°. Stir together pork and barbecue sauce in a medium bowl.

2. Bring milk to a boil in a 4-qt. saucepan over medium-high heat; gradually whisk in grits and salt. Reduce heat, and simmer, whisking constantly, 5 minutes or until thickened. Remove from heat.

3. Add butter, whisking until melted. Add egg, whisking until blended. Pour half of grits mixture into a lightly greased 11- x 7-inch baking dish. Spread pork mixture over grits. Pour remaining half of grits evenly over pork mixture.

4. Bake casserole, covered, at 350° for 25 minutes or until set. Uncover, sprinkle with cheese, and bake 10 more minutes or until cheese melts. Sprinkle with green onions. Serve immediately with additional barbecue sauce, if desired.

grocery guide:

❑ ¾ lb. barbecued pork without sauce
❑ 1 bunch green onions

Ham-and-Bacon Quiche

**MAKES: 6 TO 8 SERVINGS   HANDS-ON TIME: 30 MIN.
TOTAL TIME: 1 HOUR, 45 MIN.**

1 (14.1-oz.) package refrigerated piecrusts	1 cup chopped cooked ham
1 egg white, lightly beaten	6 large eggs, lightly beaten
Parchment paper	½ tsp. seasoning salt
6 bacon slices	½ tsp. black pepper
½ cup chopped onion	2 cups (8 oz.) shredded Swiss cheese
1 cup sliced fresh mushrooms	2 Tbsp. all-purpose flour
1½ cups half-and-half	

1. Preheat oven to 400°.

2. Fit 1 piecrust into a 9-inch deep-dish pie plate according to package directions; trim off excess piecrust around edges.

3. Unroll remaining piecrust on a lightly floured surface; cut desired shapes with a decorative 1-inch cookie cutter. Brush edge of piecrust in pie plate with beaten egg white; gently press dough shapes onto edge of piecrust. Pierce bottom and sides with a fork.

4. Line piecrust with parchment paper; fill piecrust with pie weights or dried beans.

5. Bake at 400° for 10 minutes. Remove weights and parchment paper; bake 5 more minutes, and set aside. Reduce oven temperature to 350°.

6. Cook bacon in a large skillet over medium-high heat 6 to 8 minutes or until crisp. Remove bacon, and drain on paper towels, reserving 2 tsp. drippings in skillet. Crumble bacon, and set aside.

7. Sauté chopped onion and mushrooms in hot drippings 3 to 4 minutes or until tender.

8. Stir together bacon, onion mixture, half-and-half, and next 4 ingredients in a large bowl. Combine cheese and flour; add to bacon mixture, stirring until blended. Pour mixture into crust.

9. Bake at 350° for 45 to 50 minutes or until a wooden pick inserted in center comes out clean. (Shield edges with aluminum foil to prevent excessive browning, if necessary.) Let stand 10 minutes before serving.

grocery guide:

- ❏ Parchment paper
- ❏ 1 medium onion
- ❏ 1 (8-oz.) package fresh sliced mushrooms
- ❏ 1 pt. half-and-half
- ❏ 1 (½-lb.) baked ham
- ❏ 1 (2-oz.) jar seasoning salt

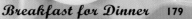

Spicy Ham-and-Greens Quiche

MAKES: 6 TO 8 SERVINGS   **HANDS-ON TIME: 25 MIN.**
TOTAL TIME: 1 HOUR

1 cup chopped baked ham	1½ cups (6 oz.) shredded pepper
1½ tsp. olive oil	Jack cheese
½ (16-oz.) package frozen	1 cup milk
chopped collard greens,	2 large eggs
thawed and drained	½ cup all-purpose baking mix*
½ cup diced onion	¼ tsp. table salt

grocery guide:

- ❏ 1 (½-lb.) baked ham
- ❏ 1 (16-oz.) package frozen chopped collard greens
- ❏ 1 onion

1. Preheat oven to 400°. Sauté ham in hot oil in a large skillet over medium-high heat 5 minutes or until browned. Stir in collards and onion, and sauté 5 minutes or until onion is tender and liquid evaporates. Layer half of collard mixture in a lightly greased 9-inch pie plate; top with ¾ cup cheese. Repeat layers once.

2. Whisk together milk and remaining ingredients until smooth; pour over collard-and-cheese mixture in pie plate.

3. Bake at 400° for 25 to 35 minutes or until a knife inserted in center comes out clean. Let stand 10 minutes before serving.

*We tested with Bisquick Original Pancake and Baking Mix.

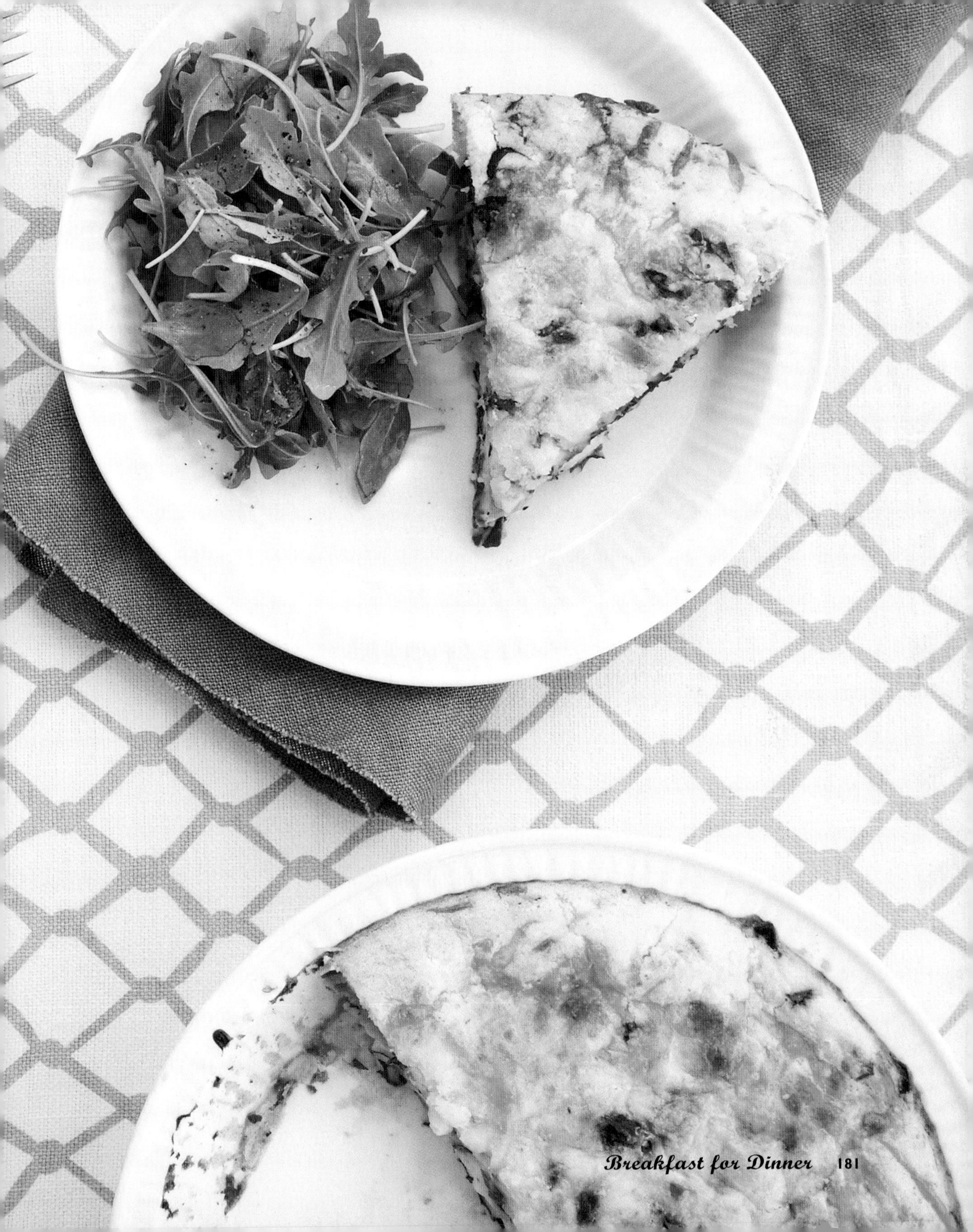

Waffles Benedict

MAKES: 4 SERVINGS
TOTAL TIME: 40 MIN.
HANDS-ON TIME: 35 MIN.

2 cups all-purpose baking mix*
1⅓ cups buttermilk
½ cup (2 oz.) shredded Parmesan cheese
2 Tbsp. vegetable oil
1 large egg
½ tsp. white vinegar
4 large eggs

1 (0.9-oz.) envelope hollandaise sauce mix*
1 Tbsp. fresh lemon juice
¼ tsp. dried tarragon
8 thin prosciutto slices (about ¼ lb.)
Garnish: chopped fresh chives

1. Stir together baking mix, next 3 ingredients, and 1 egg in a medium bowl until blended. Let batter stand 5 minutes.

2. Meanwhile, add water to depth of 3 inches in a large saucepan. Bring to a boil; reduce heat, and maintain a light simmer. Add vinegar. Break 4 eggs, and slip into water, 1 at a time, as close as possible to surface. Simmer 3 to 5 minutes or to desired degree of doneness. Remove with a slotted spoon. Trim edges, if desired.

3. Cook batter in a preheated, oiled waffle iron until golden.

4. Prepare hollandaise sauce according to package directions, adding lemon juice and tarragon.

5. Stack 2 waffles, and top with 2 prosciutto slices, 1 poached egg, and desired amount of hollandaise sauce.

   * We tested with Bisquick Original Pancake and Baking Mix and Knorr Hollandaise Sauce Mix.

Stretch Your Budget:
Substitute deli ham or country ham for the prosciutto, especially if you already have it on hand.

grocery guide:

❏ 1 pt. buttermilk
❏ 1 (16-oz.) bottle white vinegar
❏ 1 (0.9-oz.) envelope hollandaise sauce mix
❏ 1 lemon
❏ 1 (0.37-oz.) bottle dried tarragon
❏ ¼ lb. thin prosciutto slices
❏ Optional: 1 bunch fresh chives

BLT Benedict with Avocado-Tomato Relish

MAKES: 6 SERVINGS **HANDS-ON TIME: 23 MIN.**
TOTAL TIME: 23 MIN.

1	cup halved grape tomatoes	6	large eggs
1	avocado, diced	1/4	cup mayonnaise
1	Tbsp. chopped fresh basil	6	(3/4-inch-thick) bakery bread
1	garlic clove, minced		slices, toasted
2	Tbsp. extra virgin olive oil	3	cups firmly packed arugula
1	Tbsp. red wine vinegar, divided	12	thick bacon slices, cooked

1. Combine tomatoes, next 4 ingredients, and 2 ½ tsp. red wine vinegar in a small bowl.

2. Add water to depth of 3 inches in a large saucepan. Bring to a boil; reduce heat, and maintain at a light simmer. Add remaining ½ tsp. red wine vinegar. Break eggs, and slip into water, 1 at a time, as close as possible to surface. Simmer 3 to 5 minutes or to desired degree of doneness. Remove with a slotted spoon. Trim edges, if desired.

3. Spread mayonnaise on 1 side of each bread slice. Layer each with ½ cup arugula, 2 bacon slices, and 1 egg. Top with tomato mixture.

Kid Flip: Sunny-side up or sliced boiled eggs would work just as well as poached eggs for this dish.

grocery guide:
- ❏ 1 pt. grape tomatoes
- ❏ 1 avocado
- ❏ 1 bunch fresh basil
- ❏ 1 small garlic bulb
- ❏ 1 bakery bread loaf
- ❏ 1 (5-oz.) container arugula

Pancakes with Buttered Honey Syrup

MAKES: 8 SERVINGS   **HANDS-ON TIME: 30 MIN.**
TOTAL TIME: 30 MIN.

1 ¾	cups all-purpose flour	2	cups buttermilk
2	tsp. sugar	2	large eggs
1 ½	tsp. baking powder	¼	cup butter, melted
1	tsp. baking soda		Buttered Honey Syrup
1	tsp. table salt		

1. Combine flour and next 4 ingredients in a large bowl. Whisk together buttermilk and eggs. Gradually stir buttermilk mixture into flour mixture. Gently stir in butter. (Batter will be lumpy.)

2. Pour about ¼ cup batter for each pancake onto a hot, lightly greased griddle or large nonstick skillet over medium heat. Cook pancakes 3 to 4 minutes or until tops are covered with bubbles and edges look dry and cooked. Turn and cook 3 to 4 more minutes. Keep pancakes warm in a 200° oven up to 30 minutes. Serve with warm Buttered Honey Syrup.

Vanessa's Savvy Secret: Use a light hand when stirring the batter; overmixing will cause a rubbery texture. When using a griddle to cook pancakes, set the temperature dial to 350°.

grocery guide:

❑ 1 pt. buttermilk

Buttered Honey Syrup

MAKES: 8 SERVINGS   **HANDS-ON TIME: 5 MIN.**
TOTAL TIME: 5 MIN.

⅓   cup butter   ½   cup honey

Melt butter in a small saucepan over medium-low heat. Stir in honey, and cook I minute or until warm.

   * Note: Buttered Honey Syrup cannot be made ahead. The heated honey will crystallize when cooled and will not melt if reheated.

Lemon-Poppy Seed Belgian Waffles with Blackberry Maple Syrup

MAKES: 8 SERVINGS   **HANDS-ON TIME: 30 MIN.**
TOTAL TIME: 30 MIN.

2	cups all-purpose baking mix*	¼	cup butter, melted
1	to 2 Tbsp. poppy seeds		Blackberry Maple Syrup
1	Tbsp. lemon zest		Crème fraîche (optional)
1¼	cups cold club soda		Garnish: fresh mint sprigs
1	large egg, lightly beaten		

1. Stir together baking mix, poppy seeds, and lemon zest. Whisk together club soda, egg, and butter in a small bowl; gently whisk egg mixture into poppy seed mixture. (Mixture will be lumpy.) Let stand 3 minutes.

2. Cook batter in a preheated, oiled Belgian-style waffle iron until golden (about ¾ to 1 cup batter each). Serve with Blackberry Maple Syrup and, if desired, crème fraîche.

＊ We tested with Bisquick Original Pancake and Baking Mix.

Vanessa's Savvy Secret: If you don't have a Belgian-style waffle iron, use ½ cup batter for each waffle in a traditional waffle iron.

Lemon-Poppy Seed Pancakes: Prepare batter as directed. Pour about ¼ cup batter for each pancake onto a hot, lightly greased griddle or large nonstick skillet. Cook pancakes 3 to 4 minutes or until tops are covered with bubbles and edges look dry and cooked; turn and cook other side.

grocery guide:

- ❏ 1 (1.25-oz.) jar poppy seeds
- ❏ 1 lemon
- ❏ 1 (12-oz.) bottle club soda
- ❏ Optional: crème fraîche, fresh mint sprigs

Blackberry Maple Syrup

**MAKES: 2 CUPS   HANDS-ON TIME: 5 MIN.
TOTAL TIME: 5 MIN.**

½   cup maple syrup

1   (12-oz.) package frozen
    blackberries, thawed*

1   tsp. lemon zest

2   tsp. lemon juice

Combine all ingredients in a medium bowl.

  * Frozen mixed berries, thawed, may be substituted.

grocery guide:

❑ 1 (24-oz.) bottle maple syrup
❑ 1 (12-oz.) package frozen
   blackberries
❑ 1 lemon

Raspberry-Cream Cheese French Toast

MAKES: 6 SERVINGS   **HANDS-ON TIME: 20 MIN.**
TOTAL TIME: 20 MIN.

1 (1-lb.) challah bread loaf	¼ tsp. table salt
6 oz. cream cheese, softened	3 Tbsp. butter, divided
½ cup fresh raspberries	Toppings: powdered sugar,
5 Tbsp. honey, divided	additional fresh raspberries,
4 large eggs	toasted sliced almonds,
1⅓ cups half-and-half	maple syrup

1. Cut bread into 6 (1½-inch-thick) slices with a serrated knife, reserving end slices for another use. Cut a slit (about 2 inches deep and 3 inches long; do not cut in half) in one side of each bread slice to form a pocket.

2. Stir together cream cheese, ½ cup raspberries, and 2 Tbsp. honey in a small bowl. Spoon 2 heaping tablespoonfuls filling into each pocket.

3. Whisk together eggs, half-and-half, salt, and remaining 3 Tbsp. honey in a shallow dish or pie plate.

4. Melt 1 Tbsp. butter in a large nonstick skillet over medium heat. Dip 2 bread slices, 1 at a time, in egg mixture 30 seconds on each side. Cook in melted butter in skillet 1½ minutes on each side or until golden. Repeat procedure with remaining butter, remaining bread, and remaining egg mixture. Serve with desired toppings.

grocery guide:

❑ 1 (1-lb.) challah bread loaf
❑ 2 (3-oz.) packages cream cheese
❑ 1 package fresh raspberries
❑ 1 pt. half-and-half
❑ Optional: toasted sliced almonds, maple syrup

simple
sidekicks

*Pick up a deli-roasted chicken
or grill your favorite meat to serve
alongside one of these quick dishes.*

Spring Greens with Strawberries

MAKES: 8 SERVINGS   **HANDS-ON TIME: 25 MIN.**
TOTAL TIME: 25 MIN.

½	cup olive oil	1	(5-oz.) package arugula
¼	cup red wine vinegar	1	(4-oz.) package watercress
3	Tbsp. honey	1	pt. fresh strawberries, sliced
1	small shallot, finely chopped	¼	cup chopped fresh dill
1	tsp. Dijon mustard	1	avocado, cut into 1-inch pieces
½	tsp. table salt		
¼	tsp. freshly ground black pepper		

1. Whisk together first 7 ingredients in a small bowl until blended. Cover and chill until ready to serve.

2. Toss together arugula and next 3 ingredients in a large bowl. Top with avocado, and drizzle with half of vinaigrette just before serving; toss. Serve with remaining vinaigrette.

grocery guide:

- ❏ 1 small shallot
- ❏ 1 (5-oz.) package arugula
- ❏ 1 (4-oz.) package watercress
- ❏ 1 pt. fresh strawberries
- ❏ 1 bunch fresh dill
- ❏ 1 avocado

Waldorf Spinach Salad

MAKES: 6 SERVINGS   **HANDS-ON TIME: 25 MIN.**
TOTAL TIME: 25 MIN.

grocery guide:

- ❏ I small garlic bulb
- ❏ I (9-oz.) package fresh spinach
- ❏ 2 large Gala apples
- ❏ I (8-oz.) block extra-sharp white Cheddar cheese
- ❏ I bunch celery
- ❏ I (8.25-oz.) jar honey-roasted cashews
- ❏ I (15-oz.) box golden raisins

¼	cup honey		I	(9-oz.) package fresh spinach
3	Tbsp. vegetable oil		2	large Gala apples, thinly sliced
2	Tbsp. apple cider vinegar		4	oz. extra-sharp white Cheddar cheese, shaved
½	tsp. dry mustard			
¼	tsp. ground cinnamon		I	cup thinly sliced celery
I	garlic clove, pressed		I	cup honey-roasted cashews
⅛	tsp. table salt		½	cup golden raisins

Whisk together first 7 ingredients in a large serving bowl until well blended. Add spinach and remaining ingredients, tossing gently to coat. Serve immediately.

Spiced Orange Salad with Goat Cheese and Glazed Pecans

MAKES: 6 SERVINGS **HANDS-ON TIME: 20 MIN.**
TOTAL TIME: 20 MIN.

6	large navel oranges	I	Tbsp. grated fresh ginger
6	cups watercress	¼	tsp. table salt
¼	cup canola oil	½	cup crumbled goat cheese
¼	cup rice wine vinegar	I	(3.5-oz.) package roasted-
2	Tbsp. chopped fresh chives		and-glazed pecan pieces
I	Tbsp. light brown sugar		

Peel oranges, and cut into ¼-inch-thick slices. Arrange watercress on a serving platter; top with orange slices. Whisk together canola oil and next 5 ingredients; drizzle over salad. Sprinkle with goat cheese and pecans.

Gourmet Flip: You can substitute Gorgonzola cheese for goat cheese and sliced strawberries for oranges.

grocery guide:

- ❏ 6 large navel oranges
- ❏ 2 (4-oz.) packages watercress
- ❏ I (10-oz.) bottle rice wine vinegar
- ❏ I (0.75-oz.) package fresh chives
- ❏ I oz. fresh ginger
- ❏ I (4-oz.) package crumbled goat cheese
- ❏ I (3.5-oz.) package roasted-and-glazed pecan pieces

Blueberry Fields Salad

MAKES: 8 servings   **HANDS-ON TIME: 15 MIN.**
TOTAL TIME: 15 MIN.

Fresh blueberries, red onion, and tangy blue cheese rev up the flavor of this crisp green salad.

½	cup balsamic vinegar	1	small red onion, halved
⅓	cup blueberry preserves		and sliced
⅓	cup olive oil	1	cup crumbled blue cheese
1	cup toasted chopped walnuts		
2	(5.5-oz.) packages spring greens and baby spinach mix		
2	cups fresh blueberries		

grocery guide:

- ❏ 1 (10-oz.) jar blueberry preserves
- ❏ 1 (8-oz.) bag chopped walnuts
- ❏ 2 (5.5-oz.) packages spring greens and baby spinach mix
- ❏ 1 pt. fresh blueberries
- ❏ 1 small red onion
- ❏ 1 (4-oz.) package crumbled blue cheese

Whisk together balsamic vinegar and next 2 ingredients in a small bowl. Add salt and freshly ground pepper to taste. Combine walnuts, spinach mix, and next 3 ingredients in a large bowl. Drizzle with desired amount of vinaigrette, and toss to combine. Serve immediately with remaining vinaigrette.

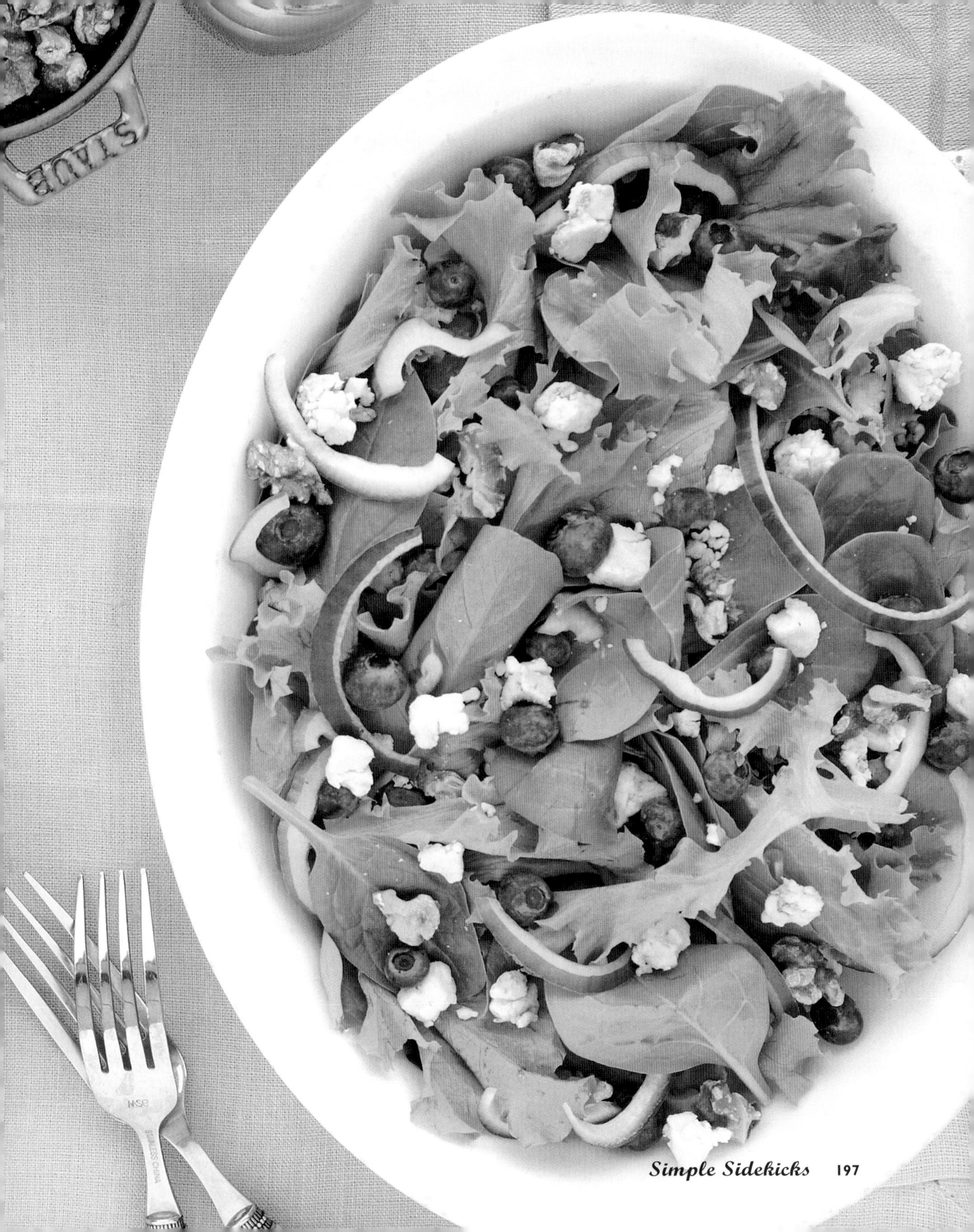

Spinach-Grape Chopped Salad

MAKES: 4 SERVINGS **HANDS-ON TIME: I2 MIN.**
TOTAL TIME: I2 MIN.

grocery guide:

- ❏ I (6-oz.) package fresh baby spinach
- ❏ I cup seedless red grapes
- ❏ I (4-oz.) package crumbled reduced-fat feta cheese
- ❏ I (I6-oz.) bottle light raspberry-walnut vinaigrette
- ❏ I (8-oz.) bag chopped walnuts

I   (6-oz.) package fresh baby spinach

I   cup seedless red grapes

¼   cup crumbled reduced-fat feta cheese

¼   cup bottled light raspberry-walnut vinaigrette

¼   cup toasted chopped walnuts

Coarsely chop spinach and grapes; toss with feta cheese and vinai-grette. Sprinkle with walnuts. Serve immediately.

Tomato-Cucumber Salad

MAKES: 8 SERVINGS **HANDS-ON TIME: 10 MIN.**
TOTAL TIME: 20 MIN.

Made with sweet grape tomatoes, this salad is tasty any time of year; you don't have to wait for summer tomatoes.

⅓ cup olive oil

¼ cup red wine vinegar

1 Tbsp. fresh lemon juice

¾ tsp. table salt

½ tsp. freshly ground black pepper

4 cups grape tomatoes, halved

2 ½ cups sliced seedless or English cucumber

¼ cup chopped fresh parsley

¼ cup thinly sliced sweet onion

2 Tbsp. chopped fresh oregano

grocery guide:

❏ 1 lemon
❏ 1 package grape tomatoes
❏ 2 English cucumbers
❏ 1 bunch fresh parsley
❏ 1 small sweet onion
❏ 1 bunch fresh oregano

Whisk together first 5 ingredients in a large bowl. Add tomatoes and remaining ingredients; toss well. Let stand 10 minutes before serving.

Green Bean Pasta Salad with Lemon-Thyme Vinaigrette

MAKES: 4 TO 6 SERVINGS   **HANDS-ON TIME: 15 MIN.**
TOTAL TIME: 30 MIN.

12	oz. uncooked casarecce pasta*	1	garlic clove, minced
½	lb. haricots verts (thin green beans), cut in half lengthwise	1	tsp. table salt
		½	tsp. freshly ground black pepper
1	Tbsp. chopped fresh thyme	5	Tbsp. olive oil
5	tsp. lemon zest, divided	1½	cups loosely packed arugula
¼	cup finely chopped roasted, salted pistachios		Toppings: additional roasted, salted pistachios; finely shredded Parmesan cheese
2	Tbsp. Champagne vinegar		
1	Tbsp. minced shallots		

1. Cook pasta according to package directions, adding green beans to boiling water during last 2 minutes of cooking time; drain. Rinse pasta mixture with cold running water; drain well.

2. Place pasta mixture, thyme, and 3 tsp. lemon zest in a large bowl; toss gently to combine.

3. Whisk together pistachios, next 5 ingredients, and remaining 2 tsp. lemon zest in a small bowl. Add oil in a slow, steady stream, whisking constantly until blended. Drizzle over pasta mixture. Add arugula, and toss gently to coat. Serve with desired toppings.

  * We tested with Whole Foods Market Organic Casarecce pasta.

Kid Flip: Substitute penne pasta for the casarecce.

grocery guide:

- ❑ 12 oz. uncooked casarecce pasta
- ❑ ½ lb. haricots verts
- ❑ 1 (0.67-oz.) package fresh thyme
- ❑ 2 lemons
- ❑ 1 (6-oz.) bag roasted, salted pistachios
- ❑ 1 (8.5-oz.) bottle Champagne vinegar
- ❑ 1 large shallot
- ❑ 1 small garlic bulb
- ❑ 1 (5-oz.) package arugula

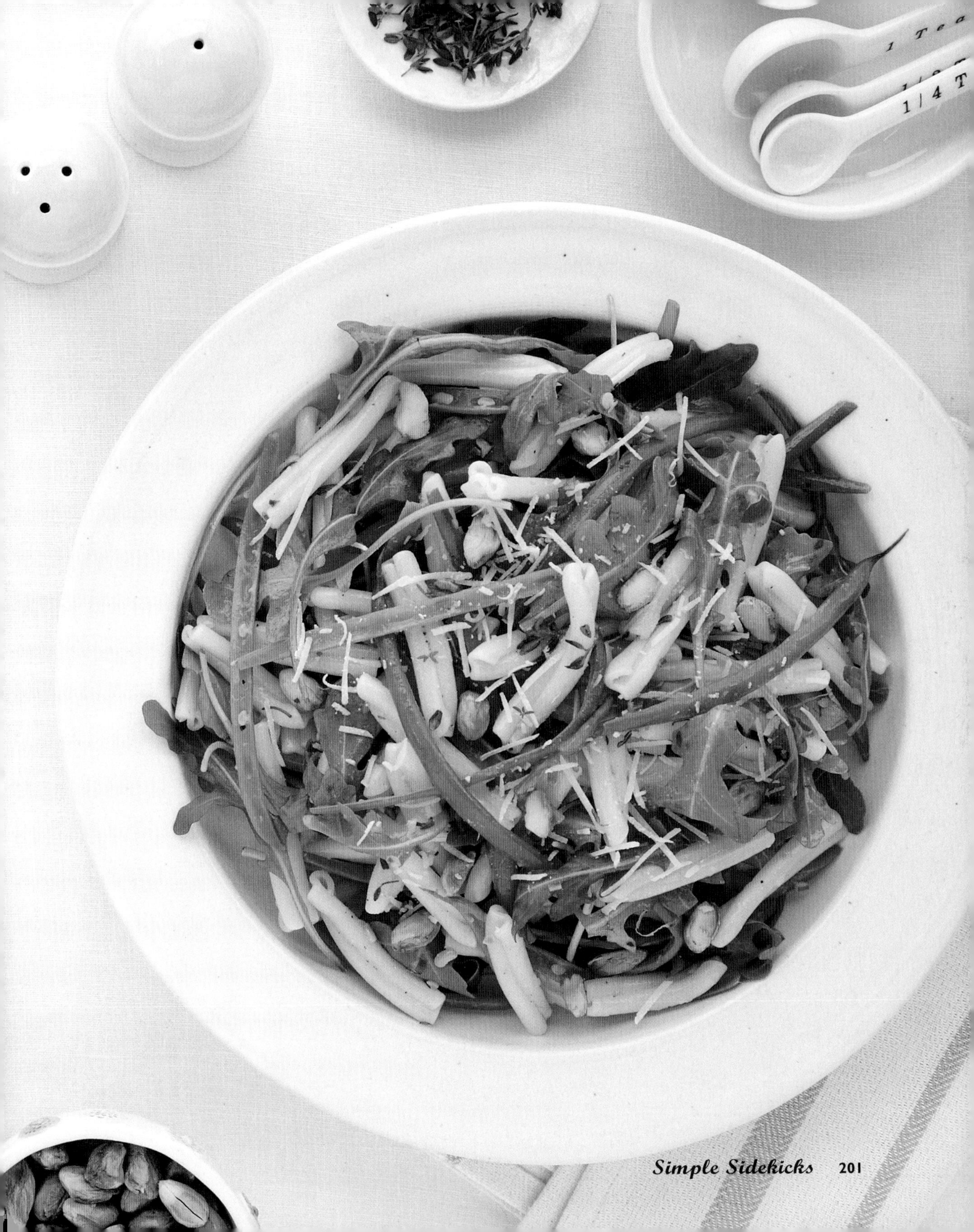

Peach-Ginger Slaw

MAKES: 8 SERVINGS   **HANDS-ON TIME: 20 MIN.**
TOTAL TIME: 30 MIN.

Turn a coleslaw recipe into a special summertime treat with chopped fresh peaches, pecans, pepper jelly, and fresh ginger. The peaches add a pleasing sweetness to the savory slaw.

3	Tbsp. pepper jelly	2	large fresh peaches,
¼	cup rice wine vinegar		unpeeled and coarsely
1	Tbsp. sesame oil		chopped (about 2 cups)
1	tsp. grated fresh ginger	1	cup toasted chopped pecans
⅓	cup canola oil		
1	(16-oz.) package shredded		
	coleslaw mix		

1. Microwave jelly in a large microwave-safe bowl at HIGH 15 seconds. Whisk in vinegar and next 2 ingredients until blended. Gradually add canola oil in a slow, steady stream, whisking constantly until well blended.

2. Add coleslaw mix, and toss to coat. Gently stir in peaches. Stir in pecans; add salt to taste. Serve immediately, or cover and chill up to 8 hours, stirring in pecans and salt to taste just before serving.

grocery guide:
- ❑ 1 (10 ½-oz.) jar pepper jelly
- ❑ 1 (10-oz.) bottle rice wine vinegar
- ❑ 1 oz. fresh ginger
- ❑ 1 (16-oz.) package shredded coleslaw mix
- ❑ 2 large fresh peaches

Roasted Baby Beets

**MAKES: 4 TO 6 SERVINGS HANDS-ON TIME: 25 MIN.
TOTAL TIME: 1 HOUR, 55 MIN.**

2 lb. baby beets	Dash of table salt
4 Tbsp. butter, cut into pieces	Dash of black pepper
1 cup vegetable broth	1 Tbsp. olive oil
¼ cup honey	Toppings: chopped hazelnuts,
2 Tbsp. apple cider vinegar	coarsely chopped fresh
3 fresh thyme sprigs	parsley, crumbled ricotta
3 fresh parsley sprigs	salata cheese

1. Preheat oven to 350°. Remove tops and ends of beets; wash beets, and place in an 11- x 7-inch baking dish. Dot with butter. Stir together broth and next 6 ingredients; pour over beets. Cover tightly with aluminum foil. Bake 1 hour and 15 minutes or until tender. Remove beets, reserving ¼ cup pan juices. Cool beets 15 minutes; peel and quarter.

2. Cook beets in hot oil in a large skillet over medium heat, stirring often, 3 to 4 minutes or until lightly browned. Pour reserved pan juices over beets; increase heat to medium-high. Cook 2 to 3 minutes or until liquid is reduced to about 1 Tbsp. Serve with desired toppings.

Vanessa's Savvy Secret: Trim the tops, but leave part of the stems to ensure the colorful pigment remains inside the beet during roasting.

grocery guide:

❏ 2 lb. baby beets
❏ 1 (0.67-oz.) package fresh thyme
❏ 1 bunch fresh parsley
❏ Optional: chopped hazelnuts, crumbled ricotta salata cheese

Quick-Start Bacon-Cheddar Mac 'n' Cheese

MAKES: 9 servings **HANDS-ON TIME: 20 MIN.**
TOTAL TIME: 20 MIN.

1⅔ cups uncooked elbow macaroni	2 oz. cream cheese, cubed
1 (12-oz.) can evaporated milk	¼ tsp. freshly ground black pepper
1 (8-oz.) block extra-sharp Cheddar cheese, shredded	¼ cup sliced green onions
6 oz. pasteurized prepared cheese product, cubed	6 cooked bacon slices, crumbled

1. Prepare pasta according to package directions.

2. Meanwhile, combine evaporated milk, cheeses, and black pepper in a large microwave-safe bowl. Microwave at MEDIUM (50% power) 8 minutes or until cheeses melt, stirring every 3 minutes.

3. Stir pasta into cheese sauce; sprinkle with green onions and bacon. Serve immediately.

Vanessa's Savvy Secret: Rather than purchasing shredded cheese, shred the cheese from a block to ensure good melting. You'll still have dinner on the table in no time thanks to a microwave-cooked sauce.

grocery guide:

- ☐ 1 (16-oz.) package elbow macaroni
- ☐ 1 (12-oz.) can evaporated milk
- ☐ 1 (8-oz.) block extra-sharp Cheddar cheese, shredded
- ☐ 6 oz. pasteurized prepared cheese product
- ☐ 1 (3-oz.) package cream cheese
- ☐ 1 bunch green onions

Hoppin' John Parfaits

MAKES: 12 servings **HANDS-ON TIME: 30 min.**
TOTAL TIME: 30 min.

1	cup uncooked basmati rice	2	green onions, thinly sliced
3	bacon slices	1	celery rib, finely chopped
1	cup chopped sweet onion	¼	cup chopped fresh parsley
1	jalapeño pepper, seeded and minced	¼	cup olive oil
2	(15 ½-oz.) cans black-eyed peas, drained and rinsed	2	Tbsp. apple cider vinegar
1	large tomato, finely chopped	1	cup (4 oz.) shredded pepper Jack cheese

1. Prepare rice according to package directions.

2. Meanwhile, cook bacon in a medium skillet over medium-high heat 10 to 12 minutes or until crisp. Remove bacon, and drain on paper towels, reserving 1 Tbsp. drippings in skillet. Crumble bacon.

3. Sauté onion and jalapeño pepper in hot drippings 3 to 5 minutes or until lightly browned; stir in black-eyed peas and 1 cup water. Reduce heat to medium, and simmer, stirring occasionally, 5 to 7 minutes or until liquid has almost completely evaporated.

4. Stir together tomato and next 5 ingredients in a small bowl. Layer black-eyed pea mixture, hot cooked rice, and tomato mixture in 12 (7-oz.) glasses. Top with cheese and crumbled bacon.

Stretch Your Budget:
Make use of those extra cans of black-eyed peas that have been sitting on the back shelf of your pantry for several months with this tasty recipe.

grocery guide:
❏ 1 (2-lb.) bag basmati rice
❏ 1 sweet onion
❏ 1 jalapeño pepper
❏ 1 large tomato
❏ 1 bunch green onions
❏ 1 bunch celery ribs
❏ 1 bunch fresh parsley

Mom's Lucky Black-eyed Peas

MAKES: 4 TO 6 SERVINGS   **HANDS-ON TIME: 15 min.**
TOTAL TIME: 8 HOURS

1 (16-oz.) package dried black-eyed peas	1 jalapeño pepper, seeded and diced (optional)
2 oz. salt pork	Garnishes: chopped green onions, cooked and crumbled bacon
1 large onion, chopped	
1 tsp. bacon drippings	
½ tsp. ground black pepper	

1. Rinse and sort peas according to package directions. Place peas in a large Dutch oven; cover with cold water 2 inches above peas, and let soak 6 to 8 hours (or see "Quick-Soak" method below). Drain peas, and rinse thoroughly.

2. Bring salt pork and 1 qt. water to a boil in Dutch oven over medium-high heat; reduce heat to medium-low, and simmer 30 minutes. Add peas, onion, next 2 ingredients, water to cover, and, if desired, jalapeño pepper. Bring to a boil over medium-high heat. Cover, reduce heat, and cook, stirring occasionally, 1 hour to 1 hour and 30 minutes or until peas are tender and liquid thickens slightly. (Uncover after 1 hour to allow liquid to evaporate, if necessary.) Season with salt and pepper to taste.

Quick-Soak Black-eyed Peas:
Place peas in a Dutch oven; cover with cold water 2 inches above peas. Bring to a boil; boil 1 minute. Cover, remove from heat, and let stand 1 hour. Drain peas, and rinse thoroughly. Proceed as directed in Step 2.

Vanessa's Savvy Secret:
For convenience, look for a 12-oz. package of sliced salt pork from Hormel. You'll need three slices.

grocery guide:
- ❏ 1 (16-oz.) package dried black-eyed peas
- ❏ 1 (12-oz.) package salt pork
- ❏ 1 large onion
- ❏ 1 jalapeño pepper
- ❏ Optional: 1 bunch green onions

Balsamic-Roasted Carrots and Parsnips

MAKES: 8 TO 10 SERVINGS   **HANDS-ON TIME: 20 MIN.**
TOTAL TIME: 1 HOUR

1 (4-oz.) package feta cheese, crumbled	½ tsp. dried crushed red pepper
½ cup chopped sweetened dried cherries	4 Tbsp. olive oil, divided
¼ cup chopped fresh flat-leaf parsley	1 ½ lb. carrots
	1 ½ lb. parsnips
1 tsp. lemon zest	2 Tbsp. light brown sugar
	3 Tbsp. balsamic vinegar
	Freshly ground black pepper

1. Preheat oven to 400°. Toss together first 5 ingredients and 1 Tbsp. olive oil in a small bowl.

2. Cut carrots and parsnips lengthwise into long, thin strips.

3. Whisk together brown sugar, balsamic vinegar, and remaining 3 Tbsp. olive oil in a large bowl. Toss with carrots and parsnips, and place on a lightly greased 15- x 10-inch jelly-roll pan. Sprinkle with salt and freshly ground pepper to taste.

4. Bake at 400° for 40 to 45 minutes or until vegetables are tender and browned, stirring every 15 minutes. Transfer to a serving platter, and gently toss with feta cheese mixture.

grocery guide:

❏ 1 (4-oz.) package feta cheese
❏ 1 (5-oz.) package sweetened dried cherries
❏ 1 bunch fresh flat-leaf parsley
❏ 1 lemon
❏ 1 ½ lb. carrots
❏ 1 ½ lb. parsnips

Pepper Jelly-Glazed Carrots

MAKES: 6 SERVINGS **HANDS-ON TIME: 20 MIN.**
TOTAL TIME: 25 MIN.

1	(32-oz.) package carrots, halved crosswise	1	(10 ½-oz.) jar red pepper jelly
1	(10 ½-oz.) can condensed chicken broth, undiluted	2	Tbsp. butter

1. Cut carrot halves lengthwise into quarters. Bring carrots and chicken broth to a boil in a skillet over medium-high heat, and cook, stirring often, 6 to 8 minutes or until carrots are crisp-tender and broth is reduced to ¼ cup.

2. Stir in pepper jelly and butter, and cook, stirring constantly, 5 minutes or until mixture thickens and carrots are glazed. Transfer to a serving dish, using a slotted spoon. Pour half of pan juices over carrots; discard remaining pan juices.

Gourmet Flip: Even the most finicky of eaters will love the savory-sweet flavor of Pepper Jelly-Glazed Carrots. To add a bit more zip to this side dish, use hot jalapeño pepper jelly instead of the regular.

grocery guide:

- ❏ 1 (32-oz.) package carrots
- ❏ 1 (10 ½-oz.) can condensed chicken broth, undiluted
- ❏ 1 (10 ½-oz.) jar red pepper jelly

Fried Confetti Corn

MAKES: 8 SERVINGS   **HANDS-ON TIME: 30 MIN.**
TOTAL TIME: 30 MIN.

8	bacon slices	1	(8-oz.) package cream
6	cups fresh sweet corn		cheese, cubed
	kernels (about 8 ears)	½	cup half-and-half
1	cup diced sweet onion	1	tsp. sugar
½	cup chopped red bell pepper	1	tsp. table salt
½	cup chopped green bell	1	tsp. black pepper
	pepper		

1. Cook bacon in a large skillet over medium-high heat 6 to 8 minutes or until crisp. Remove bacon, and drain on paper towels, reserving 2 Tbsp. drippings in skillet. Coarsely crumble bacon.

2. Sauté corn and next 3 ingredients in hot drippings in skillet over medium-high heat 6 minutes or until tender. Add cream cheese and half-and-half, stirring until cream cheese melts. Stir in sugar and next 2 ingredients. Transfer to a serving dish, and top with bacon.

Stretch Your Budget: Frozen corn can be used if fresh corn is out of season. Using the frozen is also a big time-saver.

grocery guide:

- ❏ 8 ears fresh corn
- ❏ 1 sweet onion
- ❏ 1 red bell pepper
- ❏ 1 green bell pepper
- ❏ 1 (8-oz.) package cream cheese
- ❏ 1 pt. half-and-half

Herbed Peas and Onions

MAKES: 6 SERVINGS **HANDS-ON TIME: 14 MIN.**
TOTAL TIME: 14 MIN.

1 cup sliced onion	1 tsp. lemon zest
1 Tbsp. olive oil	½ tsp. table salt
1 (14.4-oz.) bag frozen sweet peas	½ tsp. freshly ground black pepper
¼ cup chopped fresh basil or mint	Garnish: fresh basil or mint leaves

Sauté onion in hot oil in a large skillet over medium-high heat 5 minutes or until tender. Add peas; cook, stirring occasionally, 3 minutes or until peas are thoroughly heated. Remove from heat; stir in basil and next 3 ingredients.

Vanessa's Savvy Secret: To make this side dish even more quick and easy, use chopped onion from the produce department. Serve this dish with grilled salmon or chicken.

grocery guide:

- ❏ 1 medium onion
- ❏ 1 (14.4-oz.) bag frozen sweet peas
- ❏ 1 bunch fresh mint or basil
- ❏ 1 lemon

Squash-and-Onion Sauté

MAKES: 6 TO 8 SERVINGS   **HANDS-ON TIME: 12 MIN.**
TOTAL TIME: 12 MIN.

2   Tbsp. butter
2   medium-size yellow squash,
    sliced into half moons
2   medium zucchini, sliced into
    half moons
I   small onion, sliced

2   garlic cloves, minced
2   tsp. sugar
½   tsp. table salt
¼   tsp. freshly ground black
    pepper
2   Tbsp. thinly sliced fresh basil

Melt butter in a large nonstick skillet over medium heat; add squash,
zucchini, onion, and garlic, and sauté 6 to 8 minutes or until vegetables
are tender. Stir in sugar, salt, and black pepper; sauté 2 minutes.
Remove from heat; sprinkle with basil.

grocery guide:

❑ 2 medium-size yellow squash
❑ 2 medium zucchini
❑ I small onion
❑ I small garlic bulb
❑ I bunch fresh basil

Lemon Broccolini

**MAKES: 6 TO 8 SERVINGS   HANDS-ON TIME: 20 MIN.
TOTAL TIME: 20 MIN.**

1	cup (½-inch) French bread baguette cubes	2	tsp. lemon zest
2	Tbsp. butter	1 ½	lb. fresh Broccolini
1	garlic clove, pressed	2	Tbsp. fresh lemon juice
2	Tbsp. chopped fresh flat-leaf parsley	1	Tbsp. olive oil

1. Process bread in a food processor 30 seconds to 1 minute or until coarsely crumbled.

2. Melt butter with garlic in a large skillet over medium heat; add breadcrumbs, and cook, stirring constantly, 2 to 3 minutes or until golden brown. Remove from heat, and stir in parsley and lemon zest.

3. Cook Broccolini in boiling salted water to cover 3 to 4 minutes or until crisp-tender; drain well. Toss Broccolini with lemon juice, olive oil, and salt and freshly ground pepper to taste. Transfer to a serving platter, and sprinkle with breadcrumb mixture.

grocery guide:

❑ 1 (8.5-oz.) French bread baguette
❑ 1 small garlic bulb
❑ 1 bunch fresh flat-leaf parsley
❑ 1 lemon
❑ 3 bunches fresh Broccolini

Broccoli Slaw with Candied Pecans

MAKES: 6 SERVINGS   **HANDS-ON TIME: 25 MIN.**
TOTAL TIME: 1 HOUR, 25 MIN.

1 lb. fresh broccoli	1 tsp. lemon zest
1 cup mayonnaise	¼ tsp. ground red pepper
½ cup thinly sliced green onions	½ small head napa cabbage (about 1 lb.), thinly sliced*
⅓ cup sugar	½ cup golden raisins
⅓ cup red wine vinegar	1 (3.5-oz.) package roasted glazed pecan pieces
1 tsp. table salt	

1. Cut broccoli florets from stems; separate florets into small pieces using a paring knife. Peel away tough outer layer of stems; finely chop stems.

2. Whisk together mayonnaise and next 6 ingredients in a large bowl; add cabbage, raisins, and broccoli, and stir to coat. Cover and chill 1 hour. Stir in pecans just before serving.

*1 (16-oz.) package coleslaw mix may be substituted.

Stretch Your Budget: If you don't use raisins very often, you can also buy a package of 6 (1-oz.) boxes of the golden raisins so that they will remain fresh until ready to use.

grocery guide:
- ❑ 1 lb. fresh broccoli
- ❑ 1 bunch green onions
- ❑ 1 lemon
- ❑ 1 small head napa cabbage
- ❑ 1 (15-oz.) box golden raisins
- ❑ 1 (3.5-oz.) package roasted glazed pecan pieces

Roasted Green Beans

MAKES: 6 TO 8 SERVINGS   **HANDS-ON TIME: 10 MIN.**
TOTAL TIME: 25 MIN.

- 1 lb. haricots verts (thin green beans), trimmed
- 1 Tbsp. olive oil
- 1 Tbsp. butter, melted
- 1 tsp. kosher salt
- 1 tsp. country-style Dijon mustard

Preheat oven to 400°. Toss together all ingredients. Spread in a single layer on a 15- x 10-inch jelly-roll pan. Bake 15 to 18 minutes or just until tender, stirring twice.

grocery guide:

❏ 1 lb. haricots verts

Make It Snappy: Seasoned green beans may be covered and chilled up to 24 hours before baking to save time.

Balsamic-Roasted Asparagus

MAKES: 4 SERVINGS
TOTAL TIME: 16 MIN.

HANDS-ON TIME: 6 MIN.

1	lb. fresh asparagus	½	tsp. freshly ground black pepper
2	garlic cloves, minced		
1	Tbsp. balsamic vinegar	¼	tsp. kosher salt
2	tsp. olive oil	2	oz. crumbled feta cheese

1. Preheat oven to 450°. Snap off and discard tough ends of asparagus. Place asparagus and garlic on a jelly-roll pan. Drizzle with vinegar and oil; sprinkle with black pepper and salt. Toss to coat.

2. Bake at 450° for 10 to 13 minutes or just until tender. Sprinkle with feta cheese.

Gourmet Flip: If you prefer goat cheese, substitute it for feta.

grocery guide:
- ❏ 1 lb. fresh asapargus
- ❏ 1 small garlic bulb
- ❏ 1 (4-oz.) package crumbled feta cheese

Pan-fried Okra, Onion, and Tomatoes

MAKES: 8 SERVINGS **HANDS-ON TIME: 22 MIN.**
TOTAL TIME: 22 MIN.

This light and healthy Southern stir-fry brings together a merry mix of vegetables.

2	lb. fresh okra	2	Tbsp. fresh lime juice
½	cup vegetable oil	1½	tsp. table salt
1	medium-size red onion, thinly sliced	1½	tsp. black pepper
2	large tomatoes, seeded and thinly sliced	1	tsp. chicken bouillon granules

1. Cut okra in half lengthwise.

2. Pour ¼ cup oil into a large skillet over medium-high heat. Cook half of okra in hot oil, in batches, 6 minutes or until browned, turning occasionally. Remove from skillet, and drain well on paper towels. Repeat with remaining okra, adding remaining ¼ cup oil as needed. Cool.

3. Stir together onion and next 5 ingredients in a large bowl; add okra, tossing to coat. Serve at room temperature.

grocery guide:

- ❏ 2 lb. fresh okra
- ❏ 1 medium-size red onion
- ❏ 2 large tomatoes
- ❏ 2 limes

Sour Cream-and-Chive Mashed Potatoes

MAKES: 6 SERVINGS **HANDS-ON TIME: 9 MIN.**
TOTAL TIME: 29 MIN.

3	lb. baby red potatoes, quartered	¼	cup butter, softened
1½	tsp. table salt, divided	1	Tbsp. chopped fresh chives
1	(8-oz.) container sour cream	½	tsp. freshly ground black pepper
¼	cup milk		

1. Bring potatoes, ½ tsp. salt, and water to cover to a boil in a large saucepan. Cook 20 to 25 minutes or until potatoes are tender; drain.

2. Mash together potatoes, sour cream, milk, butter, chives, pepper, and remaining 1 tsp. salt until butter melts.

Vanessa's Savvy Secret: Prepare the main dish while the potatoes are boiling, so every item of your menu comes together at the same time.

grocery guide:

❑ 3 lb. baby red potatoes
❑ 1 bunch fresh chives

Oven Fries

MAKES: 4 SERVINGS **HANDS-ON TIME: 5 MIN.**
TOTAL TIME: 1 HOUR

2 large baking potatoes (1 ¾ lb.), cut lengthwise into ½-inch-thick sticks	½ tsp. freshly ground black pepper
¼ cup olive oil	¼ cup freshly grated Parmesan cheese
1 tsp. table salt	1 Tbsp. chopped fresh parsley

1. Preheat oven to 425°. Place a large baking sheet in oven for 5 minutes.

2. Toss together potatoes, olive oil, salt, and black pepper in a large bowl. Arrange potatoes in a single layer onto hot baking sheet. Bake at 425° for 50 minutes or until browned and crisp, stirring occasionally. Toss with Parmesan cheese and parsley.

Stretch Your Budget: Add any fresh herbs you have on hand, or sprinkle with a little ground red pepper for some heat.

grocery guide

❏ 2 large baking potatoes
❏ 1 bunch fresh parsley

Easy Oven Risotto

MAKES: 8 SERVINGS   **HANDS-ON TIME: 6 MIN.**
TOTAL TIME: 56 MIN.

4 ½ cups chicken broth	2 cups frozen broccoli florets,
1 ½ cups uncooked Arborio rice	thawed and drained
(short grain)	1 ¾ cups (7 oz.) shredded
¼ tsp. table salt	Parmesan cheese
¼ tsp. freshly ground black	2 Tbsp. butter
pepper	2 Tbsp. chopped fresh parsley

1. Preheat oven to 350°. Lightly grease a 13- x 9-inch baking dish. Stir together first 4 ingredients in prepared dish.

2. Bake, covered, at 350° for 35 minutes; stir in broccoli. Bake, covered, 10 more minutes.

3. Remove from oven. Add cheese and butter, stirring until melted. Sprinkle with parsley.

Kid Flip: Substitute 1 package of frozen chopped spinach for the broccoli, or omit altogether for picky eaters.

grocery guide:

❏ 1 (36-oz.) jar Arborio rice
❏ 1 (16-oz.) package frozen
    broccoli florets
❏ 1 (10-oz.) container shredded
    Parmesan cheese
❏ 1 bunch fresh parsley

dessert
in a dash

End your meal with a little
something sweet during a busy
week for a true luxury.

Tangerine Chess Pie

Makes: 6 to 8 servings **Hands-On Time: 15 min.**
Total Time: 2 hours, 18 min.

The refreshing hint of citrus in Tangerine Chess Pie tempers the overt sweetness of traditional chess pie.

1 (14.1-oz.) package refrigerated piecrusts	2 tsp. tangerine or orange zest
1 ½ cups sugar	⅓ cup fresh tangerine or orange juice
1 Tbsp. all-purpose flour	1 Tbsp. fresh lemon juice
1 Tbsp. plain yellow cornmeal	4 large eggs, lightly beaten
¼ tsp. table salt	Garnishes: sweetened whipped cream, tangerine slices
¼ cup butter, melted	

1. Preheat oven to 450°. Unroll piecrusts; stack on a lightly floured surface. Roll into a 12-inch circle. Fit piecrust into a 9-inch pie plate according to package directions; fold edges under, and crimp. Prick bottom and sides of piecrust with a fork. Bake 8 minutes; cool on a wire rack 15 minutes. Reduce oven temperature to 350°.

2. Whisk together sugar and next 8 ingredients until blended. Pour into prepared piecrust.

3. Bake at 350° for 40 to 45 minutes or until center is set, shielding edges with foil after 20 minutes to prevent excessive browning. Cool 1 hour.

grocery guide:

- ❏ Plain yellow cornmeal
- ❏ 2 tangerines or 1 orange
- ❏ 1 lemon
- ❏ Optional: whipping cream

Key Lime Pie

MAKES: 8 SERVINGS **HANDS-ON TIME: 10 MIN.**
TOTAL TIME: 20 MIN.

I (14-oz.) can fat-free sweetened condensed milk
¾ cup egg substitute
2 tsp. Key lime zest (about 2 limes)
½ cup fresh Key lime juice

I (6-oz.) reduced-fat ready-made graham cracker piecrust
I (8-oz.) container fat-free whipped topping, thawed
Garnishes: lime wedges, lime twists

1. Preheat oven to 350°.

2. Process first 4 ingredients in a blender until smooth. Pour mixture into piecrust.

3. Bake at 350° for 10 to 12 minutes or until golden. Let pie cool completely on a wire rack (about I hour), and top with whipped topping.

Vanessa's Savvy Secret: To make squeezing fresh lime juice easy, remove limes from the refrigerator up to an hour before you plan to squeeze them. Then, roll them a few times on the counter before to loosen the juices.

Cherry Berry Cutie Pies

MAKES: 8 SERVINGS
HANDS-ON TIME: 15 MIN.
TOTAL TIME: 45 MIN.

These pies are the perfect size for a weeknight after-dinner treat. They're easy to prepare and can cook while you're enjoying dinner. Served with vanilla ice cream or whipped cream, they're sure to be a favorite.

2   cups frozen blackberries, partially thawed

2   cups frozen dark, sweet pitted cherries, partially thawed

1½ Tbsp. cornstarch

1   Tbsp. brown sugar

2   Tbsp. dry red wine or purple grape juice

1   tsp. vanilla extract

⅔   cup all-purpose flour

⅔   cup granulated sugar

5   Tbsp. cold butter, cut up

1   (8-oz.) package frozen unbaked mini piecrust shells

1. Preheat oven to 425°. Toss together first 6 ingredients in a medium bowl.

2. Pulse flour, sugar, and butter in a food processor 10 to 12 times or until mixture resembles coarse sand.

3. Divide berry mixture among piecrust shells. Top each pie with ¼ cup crumb topping, pressing gently to keep topping in place. Place piecrust shells on an aluminum foil-lined jelly-roll pan.

4. Bake at 425° on lower oven rack 30 minutes or until topping is golden brown and filling is bubbly.

Vanessa's Savvy Secret: Be sure to use a jelly-roll pan rather than a regular cookie sheet so that the pies do not slide off the pan.

grocery guide:

❑ 1 (16-oz.) package frozen blackberries

❑ 2 (12-oz.) packages frozen dark, sweet pitted cherries

❑ 1 (750-milliliter) bottle dry red wine

❑ 1 (8-oz.) package frozen unbaked mini piecrust shells

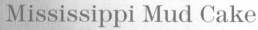

Mississippi Mud Cake

MAKES: 15 SERVINGS   **HANDS-ON TIME: 25 MIN.**
TOTAL TIME: 1 HOUR

Mississippi Mud Cake is a classic Southern sheet cake filled with marshmallows and chopped pecans and covered in a rich chocolate frosting.

1	cup butter	1	tsp. vanilla extract
4	oz. semisweet chocolate	¾	tsp. salt
	morsels, chopped	1	(10.5-oz.) bag miniature
2	cups sugar		marshmallows
1½	cups all-purpose flour		Chocolate Frosting
½	cup unsweetened cocoa	1	cup toasted chopped pecans
4	large eggs		

1. Preheat oven to 350°.

2. Microwave 1 cup butter and semisweet chocolate in a large microwave-safe glass bowl at HIGH 1 minute or until melted and smooth, stirring at 30-second intervals.

3. Whisk sugar and next 5 ingredients into chocolate mixture. Pour batter into a greased 15- x 10-inch jelly-roll pan.

4. Bake at 350° for 20 minutes. Remove from oven, and sprinkle evenly with miniature marshmallows; bake 8 to 10 more minutes or until golden brown. Drizzle warm cake with Chocolate Frosting, and sprinkle evenly with toasted pecans.

Kitchen Express Mississippi Mud Cake:
Substitute 2 (17.6-oz.) packages fudge brownie mix* for batter. Prepare mix according to package directions; pour batter into a greased 15- x 10-inch jelly-roll pan. Bake at 350° for 25 minutes. Remove from oven, and top with marshmallows; bake 8 to 10 more minutes or until golden brown. Proceed with recipe as directed.

  * We tested with Duncan Hines Chocolate Lover's Double Fudge Brownie Mix.

grocery guide:

❑ 1 (8-oz.) container
    unsweetened cocoa

Chocolate Frosting

MAKES: ABOUT 2 CUPS   **HANDS-ON TIME: 15 MIN.**
TOTAL TIME: 15 MIN.

½	cup butter	1	(16-oz.) package powdered
⅓	cup unsweetened cocoa		sugar
⅓	cup milk	1	tsp. vanilla extract

Stir together first 3 ingredients in a medium saucepan over medium heat until butter melts. Cook, stirring constantly, 2 minutes or until slightly thickened; remove from heat, and transfer to a bowl. Beat in powdered sugar and 1 tsp. vanilla at medium-high speed with an electric mixer until smooth.

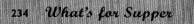

So-Easy Cherry-Fudge Cake

**MAKES: 12 TO 15 SERVINGS   HANDS-ON TIME: 16 MIN.
TOTAL TIME: 1 HOUR, 56 MIN.**

1   (18.25-oz.) package devil's
    food cake mix*
1   (21-oz.) can cherry pie filling*
2   large eggs
1   tsp. almond extract
1   cup sugar
⅓   cup milk
5   Tbsp. butter
1   cup semisweet chocolate
    morsels
Garnish: whole cherries

1. Preheat oven to 350°. Beat first 4 ingredients at low speed with a heavy-duty electric stand mixer 20 seconds; increase speed to medium, and beat batter 1 minute. Pour batter into a greased and floured 13- x 9-inch pan.

2. Bake at 350° for 27 to 30 minutes or until a wooden pick inserted in center comes out clean. Cool cake in pan on a wire rack 10 minutes.

3. Bring sugar, milk, and butter to a boil in a heavy 2-qt. saucepan over medium-high heat, stirring occasionally; boil 1 minute. Remove from heat; stir in chocolate morsels until melted and smooth. Quickly spread frosting over warm cake. Cool completely (about 1 hour).

   * We tested with Duncan Hines Moist Deluxe Devil's Food Cake Mix and Comstock Original Country Cherry Pie Filling or Topping.

grocery guide
❏ 1 (18.25-oz.) package
   devil's food cake mix
❏ 1 (21-oz.) can cherry pie
   filling
❏ 1 (1-oz.) bottle almond
   extract
❏ Optional: whole cherries

Rocky Road Chocolate Cake

MAKES: 8 TO 10 SERVINGS   HANDS-ON TIME: 25 MIN.
TOTAL TIME: 4 HOURS, 10 MIN.

Slow-cook your way to rich, chocolaty, marshmallowy goodness.

1	(18.25-oz.) package German chocolate cake mix	3 ¼	cups milk, divided
1	(3.9-oz.) package chocolate instant pudding mix	1	(3.4-oz.) package chocolate cook-and-serve pudding mix
3	large eggs, lightly beaten	½	cup toasted chopped pecans
1	cup sour cream	1 ½	cups miniature marshmallows
⅓	cup butter, melted	1	cup semisweet chocolate morsels
1	tsp. vanilla extract		Vanilla ice cream (optional)

1. Beat cake mix, next 5 ingredients, and 1 ¼ cups milk at medium speed with an electric mixer 2 minutes, stopping to scrape down sides as needed. Pour batter into a lightly greased 4-qt. slow cooker.

2. Cook remaining 2 cups milk in a heavy nonaluminum saucepan over medium heat, stirring often, 3 to 5 minutes or just until bubbles appear (do not boil); remove from heat.

3. Sprinkle cook-and-serve pudding mix over batter. Slowly pour hot milk over pudding. Cover and cook on LOW 3 ½ hours.

4. Turn off slow cooker. Sprinkle cake with pecans, marshmallows, and chocolate morsels. Let stand 15 minutes or until marshmallows are slightly melted. Spoon into dessert dishes, and serve with ice cream, if desired.

  * Note: This cake will look like it needs to cook just a little longer, but by the time the topping is set, it's ready to serve.

grocery guide:
- ❏ 1 (18.25-oz.) package German chocolate cake mix
- ❏ 1 (3.9-oz.) package chocolate instant pudding mix
- ❏ 1 (3.4-oz.) package chocolate cook-and-serve pudding mix
- ❏ Optional: vanilla ice cream

Peanut-Cola Cake

MAKES: 12 SERVINGS   **HANDS-ON TIME: 20 MIN.**
TOTAL TIME: 1 HOUR, INCLUDING FROSTING

1	cup cola soft drink	2	cups all-purpose flour
½	cup buttermilk	¼	cup unsweetened cocoa
1	cup butter, softened	1	tsp. baking soda
1¾	cups sugar		Peanut Butter Frosting
2	large eggs, lightly beaten	1	cup chopped honey-roasted
2	tsp. vanilla extract		peanuts

1. Preheat oven to 350°. Combine cola and buttermilk in a 2-cup glass measuring cup.

2. Beat butter at low speed with an electric mixer until creamy. Gradually add sugar, beating until blended. Add eggs and vanilla; beat at low speed just until blended.

3. Combine flour and next 2 ingredients in a medium bowl. Add to butter mixture alternately with cola mixture, beginning and ending with flour mixture. Beat at low speed just until blended after each addition. Pour batter into a lightly greased 13- x 9-inch pan.

4. Bake at 350° for 30 to 35 minutes or until a wooden pick inserted in center comes out clean. Cool in pan on a wire rack 10 minutes.

5. Meanwhile, prepare Peanut Butter Frosting. Pour over warm cake. Sprinkle with chopped peanuts.

Peanut Butter Frosting

MAKES: 3 CUPS   HANDS-ON TIME: 10 MIN.
TOTAL TIME: 10 MIN.

¼   cup butter
¾   cup milk
1   cup creamy peanut butter

1   (16-oz.) package powdered
     sugar
1   tsp. vanilla extract

Melt butter in a large saucepan over medium heat. Whisk in milk, and bring to a boil, whisking constantly. Reduce heat to low, and whisk in peanut butter until smooth. Gradually whisk in sugar until smooth; remove from heat, and whisk in vanilla. Use immediately.

grocery guide:

❏ 1 (12-oz.) can cola soft drink
❏ 1 pt. buttermilk
❏ 1 (8-oz.) container
   unsweetened cocoa
❏ 1 (16-oz.) jar honey-roasted
   peanuts

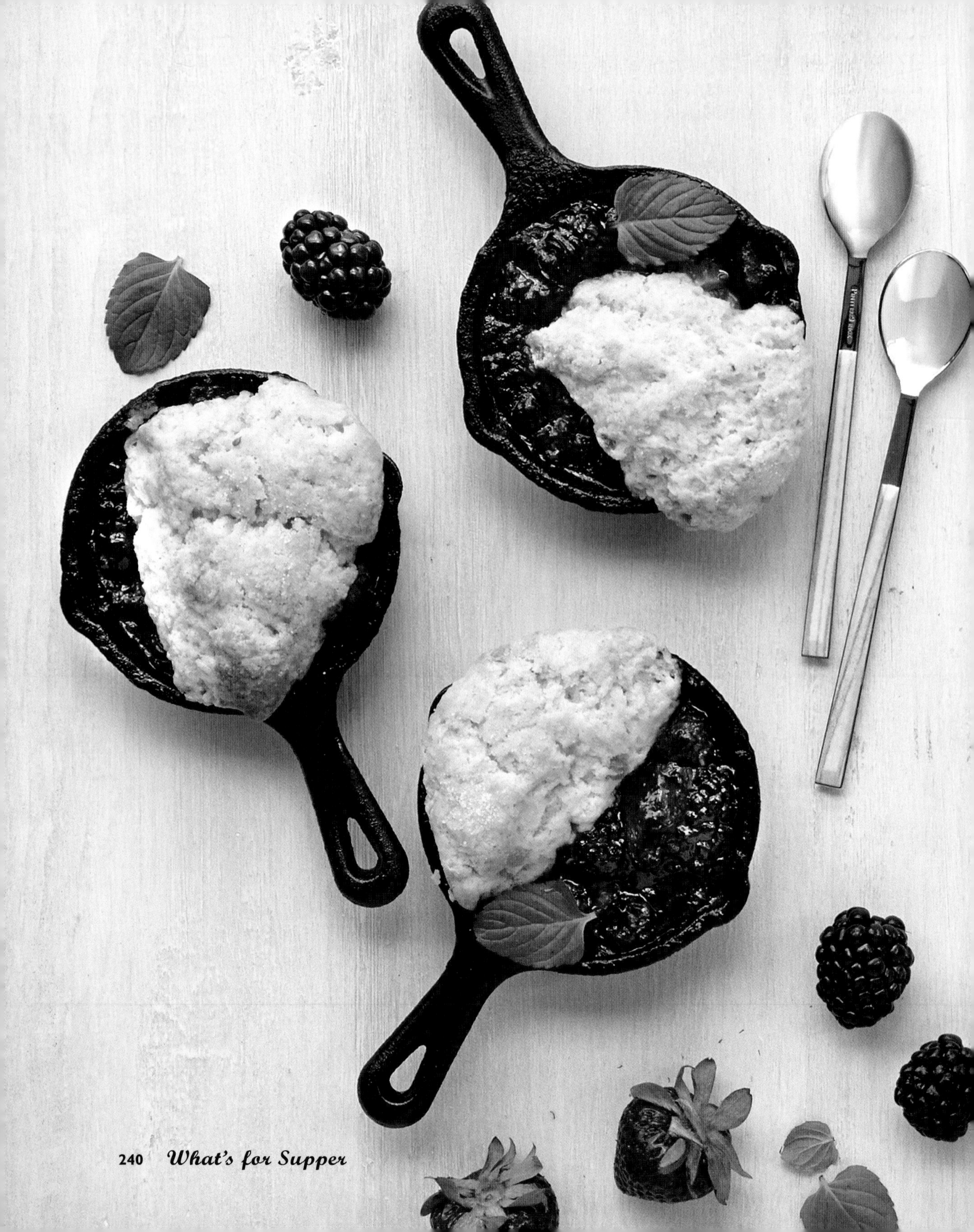

Mini Berry Cobblers

MAKES: 12 SERVINGS   **HANDS-ON TIME: 25 MIN.**
TOTAL TIME: 1 HR.

18 oz. fresh mixed berries (4 cups)
 ¼ cup sugar
 2 Tbsp. butter, melted
 1 Tbsp. cornstarch
1 ½ cups all-purpose flour
 ⅓ cup sugar
 3 Tbsp. minced crystallized
  ginger

 2 tsp. baking powder
 ½ tsp. salt
 ⅔ cup cold butter, cubed
 ½ cup buttermilk
Garnish: fresh mint sprigs

1. Preheat oven to 400°. Toss together first 4 ingredients in a medium bowl.

2. Whisk together flour and next 4 ingredients in a large bowl. Cut cold butter into flour mixture with a pastry blender or fork until crumbly. Add buttermilk, stirring just until dry ingredients are moistened. Turn dough out onto a lightly floured surface, and knead 3 to 4 times. Pat into a 6- x 4-inch (1-inch-thick) rectangle. Cut into 6 squares; cut squares diagonally into 12 triangles.

3. Arrange 12 (3 ½-inch) lightly greased miniature cast-iron skillets on an aluminum foil-lined baking sheet. Divide berry mixture among skillets. Place 1 dough triangle over berry mixture in each skillet.

4. Bake at 400° for 20 to 24 minutes or until fruit bubbles and crust is golden brown. Cool 15 minutes before serving. Serve warm or at room temperature.

Vanessa's Savvy Secret:
Use a mixture of blueberries, raspberries, blackberries, and strawberries in these charming individual desserts.

grocery guide:
❑ 18 oz. fresh mixed berries
❑ 1 (2-oz.) jar crystallized
   ginger
❑ 1 pt. buttermilk
❑ Optional: 1 bunch fresh mint

Chocolate Parfaits

MAKES: 6 SERVINGS   **HANDS-ON TIME: 20 MIN.**
TOTAL TIME: 1 HOUR, 20 MIN.

We tried using both sugar-free instant and regular pudding mixes to make these chocolate parfaits. To our surprise, we preferred the flavor of the sugar-free pudding.

1 (1.4-oz.) package fat-free, sugar-free chocolate instant pudding mix	1 (8-oz.) container fat-free frozen whipped topping, thawed and divided
2 cups 1% low-fat milk	¾ cup chocolate graham cracker crumbs (4 cracker sheets)
½ cup reduced-fat sour cream	1 Tbsp. freshly grated chocolate

1. Whisk together first 3 ingredients in a bowl until blended and smooth. Fold in 1½ cups whipped topping.

2. Spoon 1 Tbsp. crumbs into each of 6 (4-oz.) glasses, and top with ⅓ cup pudding mixture. Repeat layers with remaining crumbs and pudding mixture. Top each parfait evenly with remaining whipped topping and grated chocolate. Cover and chill at least 1 hour.

grocery guide:

❑ 1 (1.4-oz.) package fat-free, sugar-free chocolate instant pudding mix
❑ 1 (8-oz.) container fat-free frozen whipped topping
❑ 1 (14.4-oz.) box chocolate graham crackers
❑ 1 (8-oz.) chocolate bar

Double Peanut Butter Candy Bites with Granola

**MAKES: 2 DOZEN   HANDS-ON TIME: 20 MIN.
TOTAL TIME: 35 MIN.**

1 (16.5-oz.) package refrigerated peanut butter cookie dough	24 miniature chocolate-covered peanut butter cups* ¼ cup granola cereal*

Preheat oven to 350°. Shape cookie dough into 24 (1-inch) balls, and place in cups of lightly greased miniature muffin pans. Bake 15 to 18 minutes or until edges are lightly browned. Remove from oven, and press 1 miniature peanut butter cup candy into each cookie. Sprinkle each cookie with ½ tsp. granola cereal.

   * We tested with Reese's Peanut Butter Cups and Quaker Natural Granola cereal.

Peanut Butter-Caramel Candy Bites with Granola:
Substitute 24 bite-size chocolate-covered caramel-peanut nougat bars* for miniature peanut butter cups. Proceed with recipe as directed.

   * We tested with Snickers.

Peanut Butter-Caramel Candy Bites with Colorful Candies:
Substitute 24 bite-size chocolate-covered caramel-peanut nougat bars* for miniature peanut butter cups. Substitute 72 candy-coated chocolate pieces* for granola. Proceed with recipe as directed.

   * We tested with Snickers and M & M's.

grocery guide:

❏ 1 (16.5-oz.) package refrigerated peanut butter cookie dough
❏ 1 (13-oz.) package miniature chocolate-covered peanut butter cups
❏ 1 (12-oz.) bag granola cereal

What's for Supper

Rocky Top Brownies

MAKES: 32 BROWNIES   **HANDS-ON TIME: 10 MIN.**
TOTAL TIME: 1 HOUR, 35 MIN.

1 (19-oz.) package brownie mix	1 (13-oz.) package miniature
½ cup butter, melted	chocolate-covered peanut
3 large eggs, lightly beaten	butter cups, coarsely chopped

1. Preheat oven to 350°.

2. Stir together first 3 ingredients until blended. Spoon batter into a greased and floured 13- x 9-inch pan.

3. Bake at 350° for 23 minutes or until center is set. Remove from oven, and sprinkle brownies evenly with chopped candy. Return to oven, and bake 2 minutes. Cool completely on a wire rack (about 1 hour). Cut brownies into squares.

Stretch Your Budget: You can use whatever candy bars you have on hand for this recipe. It's a great way to use extra Halloween chocolate bars.

grocery guide:

❏ 1 (19-oz.) package brownie mix
❏ 1 (13-oz.) package miniature chocolate-covered peanut butter cups

Candy Bar Cookies

MAKES: 4 ½ DOZEN **HANDS-ON TIME: 30 MIN.**
TOTAL TIME: 46 MIN.

¾ cup butter, softened
1 ½ cups firmly packed brown sugar
2 large eggs
2 ½ cups all-purpose flour
¾ tsp. baking soda
½ tsp. table salt
2 tsp. vanilla extract
2 (2.07-oz.) chocolate-covered caramel-peanut nougat bars, chopped (1 cup)*

2 (2.1-oz.) chocolate-covered crispy peanut-buttery candy bars, chopped (1 cup)*
3 (1.4-oz.) chocolate-covered toffee candy bars, chopped (1 cup)*
Parchment paper

1. Preheat oven to 350°. Beat butter and brown sugar at medium speed with an electric mixer 2 to 3 minutes or until creamy. Add eggs, 1 at a time, beating until blended after each addition. Combine flour, baking soda, and salt; add to butter mixture, beating until blended. Add vanilla; beat until blended. Stir in chopped candies.

2. Drop dough by tablespoonfuls onto parchment paper-lined baking sheets. Bake at 350° for 9 to 11 minutes or until golden brown. Cool on baking sheets 2 minutes. Transfer to wire racks, and cool completely (about 5 minutes).

   * We tested with Snickers, Butterfinger, and Heath bars.

Vanessa's Savvy Secret: For an easy make-ahead cookie, use a 1¼-inch cookie scoop to make balls; place dough balls onto parchment paper-lined baking sheets, and freeze. Then, transfer the frozen cookie dough balls to a zip-top plastic freezer bag or an airtight container. Bake as directed.

grocery guide:

❑ 2 (2.07-oz.) chocolate-covered caramel-peanut nougat bars
❑ 2 (2.1-oz.) chocolate-covered crispy peanut-buttery candy bars
❑ 3 (1.4-oz.) chocolate-covered toffee candy bars
❑ Parchment paper

Bayou Brownies

MAKES: 15 BROWNIES   **HANDS-ON TIME: 10 MIN.**
TOTAL TIME: 1 HOUR, 50 MIN.

Don't think chocolate when you try these brownies. Instead, think pecans and a sweet cream cheese topping. Yellow cake mix makes the recipe extra convenient for busy cooks to whip up easily.

1 cup chopped pecans	1 (8-oz.) package cream cheese, softened
½ cup butter, melted	1 (16-oz.) package powdered sugar
1 large egg, lightly beaten	Topping: strawberry preserves
1 (18.25-oz.) package yellow cake mix	
2 large eggs	

1. Preheat oven to 325°.

2. Combine pecans, butter, 1 egg, and cake mix, stirring until well blended; press in bottom of a lightly greased 13- x 9-inch pan.

3. Beat remaining 2 eggs, cream cheese, and powdered sugar at medium speed with an electric mixer until smooth. Pour over cake mix layer.

4. Bake at 325° for 40 minutes or until set. Cool completely on a wire rack (about 1 hour). Cut brownies into squares. Microwave preserves at LOW 30 seconds; drizzle cut brownies with warm preserves, if desired.

grocery guide:

- ❑ 1 (18.25-oz.) package yellow cake mix
- ❑ 1 (8-oz.) package cream cheese, softened
- ❑ Optional: 1 (12.75-oz.) jar strawberry preserves

metric equivalents

The recipes that appear in this cookbook use the standard U.S. method for measuring liquid and dry or solid ingredients (teaspoons, tablespoons, and cups). The information on this chart is provided to help cooks outside the United States successfully use these recipes. All equivalents are approximate.

Metric Equivalents for Different Types of Ingredients

A standard cup measure of a dry or solid ingredient will vary in weight depending on the type of ingredient. A standard cup of liquid is the same volume for any type of liquid. Use the following chart when converting standard cup measures to grams (weight) or milliliters (volume).

Standard Cup	Fine Powder (ex. flour)	Grain (ex. rice)	Granular (ex. sugar)	Liquid Solids (ex. butter)	Liquid (ex. milk)
1	140 g	150 g	190 g	200 g	240 ml
¾	105 g	113 g	143 g	150 g	180 ml
⅔	93 g	100 g	125 g	133 g	160 ml
½	70 g	75 g	95 g	100 g	120 ml
⅓	47 g	50 g	63 g	67 g	80 ml
¼	35 g	38 g	48 g	50 g	60 ml
⅛	18 g	19 g	24 g	25 g	30 ml

Useful Equivalents for Dry Ingredients by Weight

(To convert ounces to grams, multiply the number of ounces by 30.)

1 oz	=	1/16 lb	=	30 g
4 oz	=	¼ lb	=	120 g
8 oz	=	½ lb	=	240 g
12 oz	=	¾ lb	=	360 g
16 oz	=	1 lb	=	480 g

Useful Equivalents for Length

(To convert inches to centimeters, multiply the number of inches by 2.5.)

1 in				=	2.5 cm		
6 in	=	½ ft		=	15 cm		
12 in	=	1 ft		=	30 cm		
36 in	=	3 ft	=	1 yd	=	90 cm	
40 in				=	100 cm	=	1 m

Useful Equivalents for Liquid Ingredients by Volume

¼ tsp					=	1 ml
½ tsp					=	2 ml
1 tsp					=	5 ml
3 tsp	=	1 Tbsp		=	½ fl oz	=	15 ml
	2 Tbsp	=	⅛ cup	=	1 fl oz	=	30 ml
	4 Tbsp	=	¼ cup	=	2 fl oz	=	60 ml
	5⅓ Tbsp	=	⅓ cup	=	3 fl oz	=	80 ml
	8 Tbsp	=	½ cup	=	4 fl oz	=	120 ml
	10⅔ Tbsp	=	⅔ cup	=	5 fl oz	=	160 ml
	12 Tbsp	=	¾ cup	=	6 fl oz	=	180 ml
	16 Tbsp	=	1 cup	=	8 fl oz	=	240 ml
	1 pt	=	2 cups	=	16 fl oz	=	480 ml
	1 qt	=	4 cups	=	32 fl oz	=	960 ml
				33 fl oz	=	1000 ml = 1 l

Useful Equivalents for Cooking/Oven Temperatures

	Fahrenheit	Celsius	Gas Mark
Freeze water	32° F	0° C	
Room temperature	68° F	20° C	
Boil water	212° F	100° C	
Bake	325° F	160° C	3
	350° F	180° C	4
	375° F	190° C	5
	400° F	200° C	6
	425° F	220° C	7
	450° F	230° C	8
Broil			Grill

index

ISBN-13: 978-0-8487-3961-4
ISBN-10: 0-8487-3961-2

Printed in the United States of America
First Printing 2013

Oxmoor House
Editorial Director: Leah McLaughlin
Creative Director: Felicity Keane
Senior Brand Manager: Daniel Fagan
Senior Editor: Rebecca Brennan
Managing Editor: Rebecca Benton

Southern Living® What's for Supper Six o'Clock Solutions
Editor: Susan Hernandez Ray
Project Editor: Emily Chappell Connolly
Junior Designer: Maribeth Jones
Director, Test Kitchen: Elizabeth Tyler Austin
Assistant Director, Test Kitchen: Julie Gunter
Recipe Developers and Testers: Wendy Ball, R.D.;
    Victoria E. Cox; Tamara Goldis; Stefanie Maloney;
    Callie Nash; Karen Rankin; Leah Van Deren
Recipe Editor: Alyson Moreland Haynes
Food Stylists: Margaret Monroe Dickey,
    Catherine Crowell Steele
Photography Director: Jim Bathie
Senior Photographer: Hélène Dujardin
Senior Photo Stylist: Kay E. Clarke
Photo Stylist: Mindi Shapiro Levine
Assistant Photo Stylist: Mary Louise Menendez
Senior Production Manager: Sue Chodakiewicz
Assistant Production Manager: Diane Keener

Contributors
Editor: Vanessa McNeil Rocchio
Copy Editors: Donna Baldone, Susan Kemp
Proofreader: Jacqueline Giovanelli
Indexer: Mary Ann Laurens
Recipe Developers and Testers: Erica Hopper,
    Tonya Johnson, Kyra Moncrief, Kathleen Royal Phillips
Interns: Frances Gunnells, Sara Lyon, Staley McIlwain,
    Jeffrey Preis, Maria Sanders, Julia Sayers

Southern Living®
Editor: M. Lindsay Bierman
Creative Director: Robert Perino
Managing Editor: Candace Higginbotham
Art Director: Chris Hoke
Executive Editors: Rachel Hardage Barrett,
    Hunter Lewis, Jessica S. Thuston
Food Director: Shannon Sliter Satterwhite
Test Kitchen Director: Robby Melvin
Senior Food Editor: Mary Allen Perry
Recipe Editor: JoAnn Weatherly
Test Kitchen Specialist/Food Styling: Vanessa McNeil Rocchio
Test Kitchen Professionals: Norman King, Pam Lolley,
    Angela Sellers
Senior Photographers:
Photographers: Robbie Caponetto, Laurey W. Glenn,
    Hector Sanchez
Senior Photo Stylist: Buffy Hargett
Editorial Assistant: Pat York

Time Home Entertainment Inc.
Publisher: Jim Childs
VP, Brand & Digital Strategy: Steven Sandonato
Executive Director, Marketing Services: Carol Pittard
Executive Director, Retail & Special Sales: Tom Mifsud
Director, Bookazine Development & Marketing: Laura Adam
Executive Publishing Director: Joy Butts
Associate Publishing Director: Megan Pearlman
Finance Director: Glenn Buonocore
Associate General Counsel: Helen Wan

To order additional publications, call 1-800-765-6400 or 1-800-491-0551.

For more books to enrich your life, visit **oxmoorhouse.com**

To search, savor, and share thousands of recipes, visit **myrecipes.com**

Cover: Poblano Chicken Tacos (page 102)
Back cover: Ham-and-Fontina Sourdough Sandwiches
    (page 74), Cheddar Pancake Egg Wraps (page 165),
    Turkey-Mushroom Lasagna (page 146), Quick-Start
    Bacon-Cheddar Mac 'n' Cheese (page 204), Mississippi
    Mud Cake (page 232)
Page 1: Shrimp Succotash (page 112)